100 PROMISES TO MY BABY

Mallika Chopra

100 PROMISES TO MY BABY

Foreword by Deepak Chopra

LOTUS COLLECTION
ROLI BOOKS

Lotus Collection

First published in US by Rodale Inc., 2005

First published in India by Roli Books, 2007
Fourth impression, 2009

The Lotus Collection
An imprint of
Roli Books Pvt. Ltd.
M-75, G.K. II Market, New Delhi 110 048
Phone: ++91 (011) 40682000
Fax: ++91 (011) 2921 7185
E-mail: info@rolibooks.com
Website: www.rolibooks.com
Also at Bangalore, Chennai, Jaipur, Kolkata & Mumbai

Cover design: Nitisha Metha
Production: Kumar Raman & Naresh Nigam

ISBN: 978-81-7436-502-6

Printed at Rakmo Press Pvt. Ltd., Okhla, New Delhi

To my mother, Rita Chopra, who embodies all the qualities of motherhood that I hope to achieve in my lifetime.

And to my precious daughters, Tara and Leela, who have unleashed in my heart and soul a love that I had never even imagined.

"*Every child that is born is proof*

that God has not given up on human beings."

—RABINDRANATH TAGORE

Contents

FOREWORD

Deepak Chopra

My medical training occurred in the midst of a revolution. It was an inner revolution that was going to change the way the world perceived healing.

Modern scientific medicine has derived formidable power from a reductionist approach to the treatment of disease. While this approach has been quite successful in eliminating major epidemics such as polio, smallpox, malaria, tuberculosis, and so on, we have in our midst new epidemics. Cardiovascular illness, cancer, addictions, AIDS, and sociopathic and psychopathic behaviors are the modern epidemics. We live in a world that is crying out in anguish and despair. Fractured relationships, dysfunctional families, broken homes, and unfulfilled dreams have become the norm. The earth itself, our mother, is grievously wounded. Every day, species become extinct; the air we breathe becomes more polluted than ever; our timber, mineral, and fossil fuel resources are increasingly depleted; the greenhouse effect is causing rising levels of the oceans; and hurricanes and floods devastate lands from Honduras to Bangladesh. Could all this be an interdependent coarising of a more fundamental disorder in the core of our being, a rift in our collective soul?

Early in my training as a physician, I realized that the reductionist approach of modern science was breeding a generation of superb technicians who knew everything about the human body, but these technicians were not healers because they knew nothing about the human soul. Spiritual wisdom traditions inform us that the essence of the human soul is pure love and that love is not a mere emotion but the ultimate truth at the heart of creation. Love heals, love renews, love makes us feel safe, love inspires us to perform great deeds, and love conquers fear, even the fear of death. Love is the glue that holds the universe together.

As a medical doctor, I learned that love is a healing force. When the emotional energy of love is exchanged between two people, their internal worlds resonate with each other. This resonance is at all levels—their biological rhythms, their sleep/wake cycles, their immune systems, and their hormone levels synchronize and lock into each other. So do their thoughts, emotions, dreams, and aspirations and the way they see and perceive the world. Dr. Thomas Lewis, a psychiatrist at the University of California, San Francisco, Medical School, refers to this phenomenon as limbic resonance. Limbic resonance, limbic regulation, and limbic revision, according to Dr. Lewis, are the most important components of the healing response. Limbic resonance is when you tune into another's inner world. Limbic regulation is when your biological functions synchronize with each other. Limbic revision is the literal rewiring of neural networks. When this occurs, the emotional parts of our brains get restructured so that we, and those we love, literally act as one soul. Our biological systems, our cognition and perception, and our emotional worlds comingle, cocreate, and coevolve, and we become healers of each other and the world.

As my children were growing, I instinctively knew that the most important thing my wife and I could do for them was to give them the self-esteem, self-assurance, and security that comes from a direct experience of the essence of one's soul. This essence is a place of love, knowingness, and bliss and a peace that surpasses understanding.

When my daughter, Mallika, became pregnant, she carried this understanding to a deeper level by consciously committing herself to 100 promises to her child. We know today that the thoughts, emotions, and intentions of a pregnant mother directly influence the physiological development of the unborn baby and that this influence continues to get reinforced when the child is born and develops and matures. This happens through play, emotional interaction, storytelling, and body language. If a mother experiences anxiety, the unborn baby reflects that through a change in heart rate, blood pressure, adrenaline, and cortisol levels. The personality of the future adult is influenced and shaped by the emotions and attitudes of the mother. Making a commitment and a promise to your child literally influences its physical and emotional development and, ultimately, its relationship to others and to the world. The mother must learn to tune in and resonate with her baby's internal world. After tuning in, she must bond so that they become one unit, and then she must participate in the continued transformation and evolution of this new human being. As she does this, she, too, transforms and evolves. Mother and baby help regulate and transform each other's internal and external worlds. Their biological rhythms, healing mechanisms, and homeostatic responses dance in response to each other, and in so doing, they sculpt and weave the tapestry of experience together.

The greatest wisdom traditions have taught us that the world is an extension of ourselves.

If every mother could create a covenant with her baby, the whole world would be transformed. Every terrorist was once a baby, and so was every saint. The world hangs precariously in the choices made by mothers.

The world was never changed or transformed by politicians, or for that matter, by scientists. The mothers of the world hold the key to the healing of our wounded planet. Let us promise ourselves that we will help them keep their promises.

ACKNOWLEDGMENTS

As the old African proverb says, it takes a village to raise a child. In many ways, writing a book is also about community, in that our ideas, inspirations, and support come from so many people. I would like to acknowledge the following people for their help in making this book a reality.

My father, Deepak Chopra, who has always given me the encouragement and confidence that I could achieve anything.

My mother, Rita Chopra, who makes life so effortless by selflessly taking care of all things and people in our world with her quiet, dedicated, and unbounded love.

My husband, Sumant Mandal, who has believed in my abilities and pushed me to achieve things that I thought would only remain dreams.

Gotham Chopra, the little brother who has become my best friend, advisor, and collaborator.

Neelam and Suresh Mandal, who have accepted me as their daughter and showered me with their love and praises.

Candice Chen and Hemant Mandal, who have become my sister and brother through their friendship and love.

Sayantani Dasgupta, Grace Rwaramba, Sarah Ross, and Edith Li—my dear friends, fellow writers, moms, and moms-to-be—whose honest feedback, stories, and reflections were invaluable to me.

Linda Lowenthal, my agent, who saw the potential for this book and gave me the confidence to take it to the next level. And Heather Jackson, my editor, whose personal journey of pregnancy and motherhood made for such a lovely exchange of ideas.

Introduction

When I found out that I was pregnant several years ago, it was one of the happiest and most exciting moments of my life. I was awed by the fact that I had a living being growing inside of me. I spent hours visualizing what my baby would look like, talking and singing to her, caressing her, and beginning to plan for our new family with my husband, Sumant.

However, as my love for my baby grew with each new day, so did my apprehension about whether or not I would be a good mother. Would I know how to take care of my baby? How would I contribute to her happiness or unhappiness? How could I make sure that she treated others well, that she felt secure, that she was on the right path? What *was* the right path? I became overwhelmed thinking about the responsibility of being a good parent.

It was at this time that I appreciated, probably at the deepest and most sincere level, how grateful I was to my parents, Rita and Deepak Chopra, for the security, patience, love, and support they had given me growing up. For much of my life, people have asked me, "What was it like growing up as Deepak Chopra's kid?" or "How did your parents teach you and your brother, Gotham, spiritual values and ideas when you were children?" Of course, for Gotham and me, our father was always just our father, and Mom was Mom. We never analyzed what it was like to grow up with them or how that was different from others.

But in the context of becoming a parent, I started to think more about the way in which my parents taught us, how they made us feel loved, and how easy it was for us to communicate. Because of my father's work as a spiritual teacher and writer and his eagerness to impart his knowledge to us, I understood at a young age how love and compassion set the foundations for everything else in life.

Gotham and I did have a wonderful childhood—not only because of the fascinating people we met, but because we were taught to look at the world with magical eyes, curiosity, and passion. Perhaps because of this background, during my pregnancy I was inspired to make commitments to myself about how I could emulate what I had learned from my parents, as well as from other family members, ancestors, friends and from my own experiences in life. My hope was to give Tara a childhood filled with wonder, magic, adventure, and mystery. And I felt intuitively that the time to start was while she still a part of me—I somehow knew she would be listening.

My desire to bond with my baby reflected what I knew scientifically, that the love and support a child feels—perhaps even in the womb—results in specific biological outcomes for health, self-respect, confidence, and behavior. And intellectually, I knew that my baby and I were connected at every level. But now, I actually began to experience my unborn baby as an extension of myself, of my body, of my mind, and of my soul.

So I started to write down promises to myself and to her. These promises were inspired by all the love and hope that I felt for her and by the anticipation of who she was going to become. As I wrote, I realized that each promise was inspired by something that I myself had actually experienced or learned. I started to write down the stories, memories, and lessons that I wanted to share with Tara as she grew up, as well as the values and intentions I myself needed to be reminded of as I faced the challenges of parenting. The result was that I could feel our bond grow and deepen as I wrote. This bond only strengthened after Tara was born and continues to evolve as she grows. I see that my love for Tara is reflected in her love for me. I know that we are constantly growing and coevolving.

Tara is now two years old. With her birth and the ensuing year, my writing project was pushed to the side as I immersed myself in actually being a mother. I have loved mothering Tara more than anything else I have ever done in my life. I have also realized that some of it comes naturally and that other parts of it are hard—very hard. You need patience, determination, and understanding. And frankly, some of the original promises that I had made to Tara were not really practical (i.e. I promise to never say no to you.)

As Tara became more interactive, learning day by day and soaking up the environment around her, I opened up my promises and decided to focus on them again. I wanted to remind myself of the commitments I had made to her when she was born, and I was inspired to write even more promises. A few weeks after I opened the promises, I also discovered that I was pregnant again! Hardly a coincidence, my passion for the project was driven by the love for Tara and my new baby, Leela, who was growing inside of me.

I have realized through this process that the bond between a parent and child is one of the most important bonds between two beings. Parenting today comes in many guises with unique challenges, from single parents to those managing divorce or separation, to parents from different cultures, adoptive parents, those who are older or younger than the norm, and those who are managing full-time jobs or daily pressures. But no matter where we fall on the parenting spectrum, we are all bonded by the role we play in shaping the innocent minds of tomorrow. As parents, we have the ability to create new global citizens who have the power to change the world. In a world that is often colored by fear and violence, this role becomes all the more important. If we all make promises to teach our children love, respect, honor, and acceptance, then we are playing our parts in creating a safer, more secure, and more nurturing world for them to live in.

My darling babies, Tara and Leela,

You have both changed my life forever. You have gifted me with your sacred presence and unleashed a love that has no limits.

I treasure the memories of feeling you grow inside my womb—the total awe of nurturing a life inside of me, the miracle of creating a new individual. You have made me feel fully alive and aware, humble, inspired, and divine.

I just need to look at you, and my heart melts with joy and love. I marvel at your every movement, your every cry, your every smile, your every word, and your every moment of existence. Despite all the uncertainty, the sleepless nights, the struggles to adjust to new ways, and the questions about whether I am raising you in the right way, I have never doubted that you are the greatest, most sacred gifts I have ever received.

I watch the world present itself to you, and I marvel at the wonder in your eyes. I look forward to our lifelong journey of discovery and helping you create endless possibilities for your wonderful futures. I am humbled day after day by the lessons that you teach me.

It is my desire that you grow up surrounded by love, joy, security, and freedom, that you feel unbounded energy and passion in every moment. I hope you sense the magic and beauty of life and are empowered to make a difference in your worlds.

In that spirit, I am making 100 promises to both of you. These are promises that you will not understand for years to come, but promises that I will keep for the rest of my life. These promises will help us grow together and spread joy and happiness to those around us.

I love you both, my little angels, with all my heart, and I am honored to share my life with you.

Your adoring mother,

Mallika Chopra

prom•ise (prä-məs) n. *A declaration assuring that one will or will not do something; a vow.*

Connections

Ways we bond
with each other and the world

1

I promise to always remember that you are my gift from God.

One morning, I was going for a walk along the ocean when I had a beautiful sensation that something was alive in me. I giggled as I imagined telling my husband, Sumant, that we were going to have a baby.

And then a wave of emotion swept over me. I felt a strong and vibrant presence at the very essence of my soul. In that moment, I felt Daddy, my dearest grandfather, in my heart. Daddy had passed away three months earlier, but I felt his spirit bless his first great-grandchild in that moment by the water.

Daddy once told me that the following poem by Jalal-al-Din Rumi always reminded him of how he felt about his grandchildren. As I embark upon my own journey as a parent, it resounds even more with the emotion I have always had about becoming a mother and discovering the magic of my children.

The Alchemy of Love

By Jalal-al-Din Rumi

You come to us
From another world

From beyond the stars
And void of space.
Transcendent, Pure,
Of unimaginable beauty,
Bringing with you
The essence of love

You transform all
Who are touched by you.
Mundane concerns,
Troubles and sorrows
Dissolve in your presence,
Bringing joy
To ruler and ruled
To peasant and king

You bewilder us
With your grace.
All evils
Transform into
Goodness.

You are the master alchemist.

You light the fire of love
In earth and sky
In heart and soul
Of every being.

Through your loving
Existence and nonexistence merge.
All opposites unite.
All that is profane
Becomes sacred again.

2

I promise to always cherish the moment you came into the world.

About six weeks before Leela, our second child, was due, it suddenly dawned on me that she would be in my arms very soon. I tried to remember how I felt when I was at this stage with Tara, but the emotions were quite different this time. There was less anxiety about the unknown and more excitement about all the joys and treasured moments that were yet to come. There was also nostalgia already because I knew that Leela's infancy would pass before our eyes in a flicker of a moment.

In the middle of the night, I'd lie awake as she moved inside of me. The miracle of being so intimate with this other being is indeed one of the most spiritual experiences I have ever had. I remembered watching Tara after she was born and recognizing her movements from those I had felt inside of me. I envisioned the familiarity I would soon observe when Leela was in my arms.

With my first pregnancy, I got lists of what I needed from friends and only imagined how I might use those things on Tara. It was such a joy and many times a struggle, to discover the little secrets of caring for my baby. For Leela, those utilitarian items—such as washcloths and nail clippers—would have so much meaning.

My heart would flutter with anticipation, joy, and nostalgia once again.

I replayed the challenges that I had with Tara—the sleepless, exhausting nights; the struggles with breastfeeding; and the questioning and trying to understand why she was crying—but they all faded into the background as I remembered those breathless moments of gawking at her in utter amazement.

I thought about what it would feel like to have another baby in my arms. I stroked my belly and hummed quietly to myself, focusing all my loving energy to little Leela's burgeoning soul. I thought about what she would look like, how she would smell, and how she would feel.

What a wonderful and magical journey awaited us! I could not wait to welcome her into our world.

Reflection

THINK ABOUT THE MOMENT you realized you were pregnant. What was your first thought? Did you have a vision of your baby? How has this vision changed as your pregnancy has progressed or your baby has grown?

3

I promise to help you know
that we are always together.

There will be times when you are scared, lonely, and sad and when I will not be there to hold you. I will not be able to pat you back to sleep, to wipe away your tears, to sing you a song, and to give you little kisses to make you smile again.

There will be times when you may fall and hurt yourself and I cannot kiss away your wound and make it all better.

There will be times when someone may say something that hurts you, and I am not there to tell you that their judgments reflect their own insecurities.

And there will be moments when I will not be able to sense your needs just by looking at you or hearing the tone of your cry.

But know that you will never be alone and that I will always be there for you. When you need me and I am physically not there, put your attention on your heart, and you will feel my presence. You will remember then. You will feel the warmth of my embrace, you will hear the song of my voice, and you will know that I love you.

We are bonded now forever, and never again will we find ourselves truly alone.

4

I promise to keep an open heart and mind as our relationship changes and evolves.

When I first met Sumant, we had a thrilling courting period. There was an instant connection, and I would wake up every morning just waiting for his call or a chance to see him.

Our first year of marriage, like most, faced many challenges, confrontations, frustrations, and questioning. But it was also a time of getting to know each other more intimately and building a more solid base for our relationship. It was a time when we were enamored with love and with each other, and the magic of it all made the challenges much easier.

Over the next five years, our lives changed dramatically as we moved from India to the United States, returned to business school, started our professional careers, and really began to live our life together. Our puppy love had evolved into the deepest of friendships and respect, and we both pushed each other to achieve our individual and our shared dreams.

Having children has taken our relationship to an entirely new level. We share a bond that is sacred; we have created new life, new beings together. We feel older, more responsible, and more serious about our lives and each other. We look at these miracles, our children, whom we have created together. They are a symbol of our love, totally dependent on us and trusting of us. I have fallen in love with Sumant over and over again as I watch him be a father.

I look at other relationships in my life, and I appreciate how they have evolved over time. My parents, who once were my sole caretakers, are now my close friends. I watch them interact with their grandchildren and see how they continue to grow as individuals and as a couple. My brother has shifted from being the often annoying but lovable younger sibling to my dear friend and creative and professional collaborator. With friends, some relationships have evolved as our lives have changed, while others remain special because of history and memorable times together.

And now, I begin a new journey of building relationships with my children. These, too, I know, will change with the years, and we will face many joyous moments combined with tense ones. But it is a journey I will cherish at every turn, because it will be the most precious journey in my lifetime.

5

I promise to trust my own instincts when caring for you.

When Tara was born, I wanted to hold her all the time. I loved her warmth, her smell, watching her expressions, and just feeling her in my arms. When she was not in my arms and started crying, I would pick her up in an instant to stroke, kiss, and comfort her. I could not bear to hear her cry. People would tell me that I was fondling her too much and that she would get spoiled. They said it was good for her lungs to cry and for her to get more independent. I could not relate to what they were saying. Why would I not want to spoil my child? Why would I want to let her cry and learn to feel alone?

As the months passed, Tara continued to stay close to me at all times. She went through phases of extreme stranger anxiety. When Tara cried, people would tell me to let her deal with the fear rather than pick her up and calm her. They said I would exhaust myself and that Tara would not learn to deal with others. But again I could not relate to their advice. Tara's fear was real, and she found comfort in my arms. I wanted her to know that I was next to her, guiding her, and helping her discover the world.

Tara began sleeping with Sumant and I when she was six months old, after a trip to India where she shared a bed with us. When we returned and Tara refused to sleep in her crib, people would tell us that if we let her cry it out she would adjust quickly. I am sure she would have, but neither of us could tolerate letting her cry it out. More important, we loved having Tara in our bed. Her warm body, her soft breathing, her baby smell, her movements—all these gave us such a feeling of love and comfort. Sumant and I could not imagine sleeping without her. But again, people continued to warn us that we would never get her out of our bed and we would have to force her to do it. Again, I questioned their words. Why would I want to force her? She felt secure being with us. We would be lost without her, and surely soon enough she would want to sleep by herself. Her presence with us was one of the most special and warm times in our lives. We could only treasure it.

Tara is now almost two-and-a-half years old, and she is confident, secure, and happy. Already she hardly lets me hold and cuddle her anymore because she is too busy running around and playing with her toys and friends. She is no longer fearful of strangers, but curious to talk and learn from people. Tara still sleeps with us, but every once in a while, she will tell me that she wants to go to sleep in her room in her bed. On those nights, I have to hold back from telling her no, because I would so much prefer that she sleep with us.

People continue to give me advice and tell me that I am doing something wrong. I listen politely, but I know that if I follow my heart, I am building bonds between ourselves and the world so that we will both be happy and secure.

Reflection

THINK ABOUT A LESSON or truth you have always needed to learn that your baby may be able to teach you as no one else ever could.

6

I promise to have a conversation with you that will last a lifetime.

I began to talk to Tara the moment I knew I was pregnant. I did not know if she could hear me, but I sensed that my loving thoughts would nourish her embryo and let her know that she was treasured.

When I saw or heard something beautiful, I would gently pat my stomach, wanting somehow to share my joy with her. When I was alone in the house, I would tell her about what was going on or what I was feeling. I would hum to her when I went for a walk or choose some of my favorite poetry to read to her before we went to sleep. I would make Sumant, who is very self-conscious about these sorts of things, talk to her as well. He would do so awkwardly, but somehow I made him do it nonetheless. At times, I felt quite silly about the extent I went to communicate with this little fetus inside of me, but for me, it was a way to bond with my baby who still seemed like a concept at times. It was a way in which I could introduce and welcome Tara to our lives.

When Tara was born, she recognized our voices. She had heard our chatter and humming and our whispers about how much we loved her. And when Tara was out in the world in our arms, we just continued the dialogue we had been having all along.

Tara and I talk constantly; my two-year-old daughter is a little chatterbox who needs to comment on everything that is going on around us. A friend of mine once observed that I talk to her as I would talk to a girlfriend, rather than to a little toddler. I think this has just become our rhythm of communication. I want to share my feelings and thoughts with Tara, and in turn, she responds. I am never lonely when Tara is with me because we are used to sharing our thoughts with each other.

When I was pregnant again, I started a dialogue with Leela that included Tara, as well. We read Leela books together, and we discussed how all of our lives would change when she arrived. Tara would pat my belly and talk to her little sister, telling her stories about her family, friends, toys, and favorite television shows. Both Tara and I would coax Sumant to talk to Leela, and he could not deny us this simple pleasure.

It is so special to know that my daughters—Tara and Leela—are now my lifelong partners and friends, who I will always be able to talk to and share my joys and sorrows with. As parents, if we talk with our children from the very beginning, we can build a bond and a conversation that will last a lifetime.

Reflection

WRITE DOWN A PROMISE about how you would like to connect with your baby—physically, emotionally, and spiritually.

7

I promise to foster your bond with the generations before and after you.

When my father was young, he and his little brother were the closest friends. Mimicking the mythological stories of the classic Indian text, the Ramayana, they were often referred to as Ram and Lakshman, who represented quintessentially loyal brothers.

One day, when they were about twelve and ten years old, my father and his brother went to the market with pocket money that they had been saving for weeks and bought a BB gun. They knew that their parents would be angry over the purchase, and they reveled in the secrecy of the whole transaction. They went to the park and began target practice. Feeling very grand about their adventure, they decided that one brother would stand under a tree with an apple on his head, and the other would try to shoot the apple off his head. My father volunteered to stand in position first, while my uncle took the first shot.

The little bullet missed its mark and instead went straight into my father's chin. As my father reeled over in pain, my uncle ran to him, wondering what he should do. His immediate thought was to run home, admit all, and tell their father about the accident. But my father held him back. The pain was nothing compared to the wrath they would face from Daddy.

So instead they went to a friend's house, snuck in through the back entrance, and had a servant clean the wound, leaving the bullet inside and putting a bandage on his chin. When they returned home and their parents demanded to know what had happened, they both acted casually, telling them that there was nothing to worry about and that they had shown it to their friend's father, who was also a doctor. My grandfather looked at my father and uncle suspiciously, sensing that they were up to no good, but he let them get away with whatever mischief they were up to for the time being.

My father writhed in agony at night, and my uncle found medication to give him. Despite all the pain, they decided that they must remain loyal to each other and were somehow able to cover up his ailment from their parents' suspicious, all-seeing eyes. Each one was fearful that if they told my grandfather, the other would get into trouble—my father for being the elder brother who led his younger brother astray, and my uncle for being the one who fired the shot.

Finally, after several days, the wound got infected, and there was no alternative. They both sheepishly approached my grandfather and asked him to look at the wound. As my grandfather took off the bandage and cleaned the wound, he gasped when he found the tiny bullet in the cleft of my father's chin. But he did not scold him or ask any questions. Rather, he decided to respect their loyalty to each other and quietly took the bullet out and cleaned the wound.

8

I promise to dance and sing and play with you for a lifetime.

There is a Native American tradition that encourages an individual to ask the following question when considering any action or word. "Will it honor the parents, the parents' parents, and the parents' parents' parents? Will it serve the children, the children's children, and the children's children's children?"

Such a sentiment creates an integral bond between each one of us and those who have come before and those who will come after. We become connected to every other creature in the universe, and we think of our existence as part of a continuum that links the present with the past and the future. It is a very powerful spiritual concept that creates a universal, timeless, and meaningful purpose for why we are here and what we can achieve.

With this notion of thinking about our existence in the context of others, I find that I am much more cognizant of how my experiences are reflections of those who came before me. Others have faced the challenges that I have faced, felt the hurts and loves that I feel, and overcame obstacles so that I can have opportunities that they never had. I can appreciate and cherish our evolution as individuals who are part of a greater continuum, and I know that I am connected to a universe that will support me.

I am also aware of how my decisions will affect those who come after me. As a mother, my immediate need has been to create a secure, happy, and emotionally rich environment for my children. But as a mother for generations to come, I find that my responsibility to the earth, to other peoples and cultures, to technology, to creativity, to art, to knowledge, and to peace is so much more significant. I seek to create opportunities for my children and all the other children who will follow through the generations.

In turn, the present moment becomes so much more dynamic, relevant, and purposeful. As parents, our actions today have more meaning and purpose, and we can sense our important place in history. With such a knowledge and responsibility, our existence itself becomes so much more timeless and significant.

9

I promise to remind you of the times
we have danced, sung, and played together.

I had a dream the other night about you and me, my baby.

We were together in a small village, surrounded by family and friends, who were singing and dancing, celebrating with smiles on their faces and joy in their steps. There were lights and music and platters of food and drink. You were my older sister, holding me in your arms and taking me from one smiling face to another. I remember stroking your face, giving you a kiss, and realizing that the love we share now has been fostered over many, many lifetimes.

And now I can imagine all the moments that we will share together for millennia to come. I see us embarking on a journey, full of hope, adventure, anticipation, and optimism. I see us as young puppies born together in a warm litter, growing up side by side, playing with a soft furry ball, and sleeping together in a small basket. I see us as an old couple, comforted by each other's love and at peace with the world. I imagine you as my teacher, who is there to support me in times of sorrow and to smile at me when I have achieved success. You and I are two birds flying together in a clear, warm, blue sky, our movements synchronized in a cosmic dance. Over and over, we play different roles, with different costumes, different temperaments, and in different places. We fight and laugh and play and scream and dance, but we are there, discovering ourselves, each other, and the universe in our many guises.

And then I see us as two stars in a galaxy of sparkling light, as the stem and bud on a beautiful rose, and as raindrops that fall in a lush jungle. I see you as water gushing down a mountain stream, and I feel myself racing you to reach the wide expanse of the ocean. I see us as two clouds blowing across the sky and as the fire of the sun warming up the planets below us.

And though I know that we have been together and have lifetimes yet to share, I remain in total awe of you. I love you as if for the first time, and I anticipate all the moments where we will be reacquainted with each other over and over again.

We have a bond as mother and child that is timeless, infinite, and pure. Let us always cherish this love that will keep us connected for eternity.

10

I promise to show you the connection between you and the universe.

Once upon a time, there was a brilliant star millions of miles away. Her name was Tara. She was warm and bright and emanated love and happiness to the rest of the galaxy. The other stars and moons and planets and the entire universe loved and depended on Tara.

Tara had one wish. She wanted more than anything else to see herself. Tara did not have any eyes, and without eyes she could not see. One night, Tara thought really hard. She asked herself, "How can I see myself?" She thought of all the ways in which she might be able to obtain eyes. Finally, she came up with a brilliant idea.

Excitedly, Tara breathed deeply and sent her bright light streaming across the universe. It was the most spectacular sight the galaxy had ever seen. The other stars, moons, and planets celebrated, and the black skies were filled with shooting stars and warm hues from the moons and planets that reflected Tara's brilliant light.

One of Tara's beams of light landed on planet earth, which was filled with luscious rain forests, flowing waters, snow-capped mountains, and fields of colorful flowers. Planet earth was always happy to receive the light and warmth from the stars, and she smiled as she welcomed Tara.

An apple tree was just waking up when she caught Tara's light. She quickly consumed its energy and started to grow delicious, juicy apples. More and more apples grew on the tree, and Tara was proud that her light had created such wonderful fruit.

On a beautiful spring day, a young woman was walking through the orchard. As she passed by the apple tree, a ripe apple fell across her path. The young woman picked it up and admired its vibrant color and its shiny skin. She bit into the apple, and it was the most delicious fruit she had ever tasted. The young woman ran back home to share the apple with her husband. Tara smiled up in the skies as she sensed how happy the young woman and her husband were as they ate the precious fruit.

Soon, the young woman realized that the energy of the apple had planted a new seed inside of her. But this was not the seed of an apple; it was the seed of a brand new baby. The young woman could feel her baby growing inside of her, and she was very happy. When the baby was born, it was the most beautiful baby the young woman and her husband had ever seen. The baby had the biggest, most innocent, and most brilliant eyes, and they literally shined with light. The young woman and her husband named the baby Tara because her eyes lit up the faces of everyone who looked at her. Up above in the skies, Tara, the star, celebrated because now she could see herself through the baby's eyes.

Every night, baby Tara looked at the stars in wonder. She giggled and cooed and talked to them. Her favorite star was the brightest one in the sky. Baby Tara watched that star and thought about how beautiful the star was. She would blow her star a kiss before saying good night, and the star smiled back at her, emitting a flicker that only baby Tara could see.

Through this nightly ritual, baby Tara knew in her soul that she was part of a greater universe and a profound spirit. She was connected to the stars, the sun, the earth, and the wind. Her spirit was as infinite, free, and bright as the stars that lit up the night sky.

Reflection

MAKE A COMMITMENT to share stories, poems, and insights with your child about how he or she is connected to other people, the earth, the universe, and a greater spirit.

Hopes

How I wish to serve as your parent

11

I promise to hold you,
but never hold on to you.

When you look at me with your big eyes, searching for a hug, a kiss, comfort, and security, my heart melts with joy. I am there in an instant, knowing that today you turn to me for everything. I yearn to hold you, protect you, and nurture you. And while it makes me whole to meet your needs, I must constantly remind myself that I am really only your guide for a short time. You are on your own journey, a bud that will blossom into its own brilliant flower.

I know there will come a time when you will no longer look to me for all your needs, when you must search for your own answers, when you will want to wander around the world and collect your own treasures. I know there will come a time when I have to let go and admit that you are old enough to make your own decisions and determine your own actions.

I promise you that I will let go and give you the freedom to grow and become your own person. And whenever you want my advice, my embrace, and my smile, I will be there for you. I will always answer your call, and I will always be there as an anchor when you need me. And while I know at times it will be hard for me to hold back, I will respect your freedom and give you wings to fly freely with confidence, joy, and security.

On Children
from *The Prophet*

By Kahlil Gibran

And a woman who held a babe against her bosom said, Speak to us of Children.
And he said:

Your children are not your children.
They are the sons and daughters of Life's longing for itself.
They come through you but not from you,
And though they are with you yet they belong not to you.
You may give them your love but not your thoughts.
For they have their own thoughts.
You may house their bodies but not their souls,
For their souls dwell in the house of tomorrow, which you cannot visit, not even in your dreams.
You may strive to be like them, but seek not to make them like you.
For life goes not backward nor tarries with yesterday.
You are the bows from which your children as living arrows are sent forth.
The archer sees the mark upon the path of the infinite, and He bends you with
      His might that His arrows may go swift and far.

Let your bending in the Archer's hand be for gladness;
For even as He loves the arrow that flies, so He loves the bow that is stable.

12

I promise to try to teach you through example, not just words.

When I was ten years old, my parents started meditating.

In the weeks following their introduction to meditation, our family life changed in quite dramatic ways. My father, who had smoked frequently, no longer took his regular walks to escape the house and get his secret drag. My parents, who previously had argued over my father's tendency to drink too much when they went out, no longer ordered the regular scotch or bottle of wine at dinner. They began to spend more time together, going for walks and exercising, and laughing more. They were more patient with us, less serious about trying to discipline us, and they spent more time talking with us rather than telling us what to do. They were generally happier, and it was more fun to be around them.

My parents never told my brother and I that we should start meditating. Rather, I remember telling them I wanted to learn. I wanted to do what they were doing and to share in their newfound experience. At ten, I did not have any dramatic life experiences, but meditation was something I wanted to do because I saw how happy it made my parents.

As I grew up, there were many times that I would forget about meditation, or months would go by where I just wasn't interested in doing it. My parents never told me to meditate. They just welcomed me to join them whenever I wanted to. In this way, my parents let me make my own decisions about what I wanted to do and how I wanted to shape my own life and destiny.

As a parent, it is challenging and difficult to let our kids make their own decisions because we often feel that we know what is best for them. To truly empower our children to feel confident and secure with their choices, we have to give them the right to make their own choices and believe that we, as parents, are setting good examples for them to follow.

Reflection

THINK ABOUT THINGS that you do that your child will learn from. What kind of example would you like to set?

13

I promise to inspire you to love and nurture your body.

I am known among friends and family for my terrible eating habits. People who look at me through the windows of "Deepak Chopra's daughter" are often shocked when I order a Coke and a chocolate chip cookie for lunch, instead of a soybean or vegetarian delicacy.

When it was time to start giving Tara solid foods, I was adamant that I would not let her mimic my eating habits. I made every effort to feed her fruits and vegetables, and in the beginning, when she had no choice, she took them relatively easily. However, as Tara became more aware of her sense of taste and more communicative about her likes and dislikes, I realized that she was watching what I ate and adapting a pattern similar to mine.

Then one day, Tara surprised me at the grocery store's checkout counter by asking me for M&M's. At one-and-a-half years old, Tara had been observing my habit of buying and eating chocolate at the checkout counter, and this had become part of her routine, as well. Tara would give me the biggest, most loving smile every time I offered her chocolate, and she began saying, "Tara and Mama love chocolate!" As endearing as it was, I was guilt-ridden that my daughter already had the sweet tooth that I have struggled with for so many years.

As a parent, I knew that I had to make a change in my eating and exercise habits because unless I showed Tara healthy habits, she had no power at such a young age to do it on her own. I realized that we had to cook more at home, eat more fruits and vegetables, sit down to dinner, and make healthy eating habits an integral part of our lifestyle. It pains me at times to force spinach down my throat, but Tara is always watching me eat, so I do it with a smile. I struggle to come up with creative recipes that will incorporate nutrients that she and I can enjoy. Sometimes it takes effort to get Tara to try something new, but her innocence allows her to make the changes much easier than I can. I also took the next step to focus on our overall well-being as a family by playing outside more, running and kicking balls, and doing yoga and meditation together in the mornings.

The end results will last both of us a lifetime. Together Tara and I will have more energy, vitality, immunity, clarity, and vibrancy. Together we are more prepared to prevent sickness and fight off disease. I will forever be grateful to Tara for changing the way in which I treat my own sacred body.

14

I promise to try not to criticize you,
even if I disagree with your actions.

Growing up, my brother, Gotham, and I were often the subjects of our father's experiments and philosophies. As young, innocent guinea pigs, we were exposed to everything from Ouija boards to hypnosis techniques (for giving up my addiction to chocolate), to memory and vocabulary tricks, and other sorts of practices.

One of the most useful and powerful tools my father taught us was the three Cs: No criticizing, complaining, or condemning. As young kids, Gotham and I made it a game to see how long we could go without expressing negative sentiments about people, places, or circumstances. Little did we realize the power that such a mental dialogue had in shaping our outlooks on the world. By not criticizing, we realized that there is most often a deeply rooted reason for someone's behavior. We learned that criticism was more a reflection of our own insecurities or unhappiness, rather than the fault of the other person. By not complaining, we learned to take responsibility and control of our circumstances. We were empowered to make changes in our environment because there was no one to blame for our own unhappiness. By not condemning, we learned that finding fault with another person did not solve any problem or improve a situation. Rather, our world was one that was controlled and shaped by us, not controlled by the people, places, and things that surrounded us.

As we grew older and life became more complicated, the game turned into a tool for empowerment, balance, and power. I remember a particular day in which Gotham, Sumant, and I were traveling back from Miami. We had challenged each other that morning to see who could go the longest without defaulting on the three Cs. Of course, the day began with a missed flight, resulting in a five-hour wait at the airport. A glass of soda soon spilled on my lap, and Sumant's computer's battery died, preventing him from completing a homework assignment that was due the next morning. Gotham was afflicted with a "sneeze attack" and found his eyes red and dry from his continuous sneezing. What should have been a simple journey from Miami to New York lasted more than twelve hours, and at every turn there was a reason for us to be angry, miserable, and sorry for ourselves. However, our commitment to not utter a negative comment actually made the journey fun, because we were able to laugh at the funny circumstances we found ourselves in, rather than get frustrated and suffer the long journey with angry, pounding hearts.

Reflection

SPEND A DAY NOT criticizing, complaining, or condemning anyone or anything.

15

I promise to help you see that you are perfect just the way you are.

One morning as Sumant was getting Tara dressed, she told him in very clear language that she did not want to wear her tights. "I look fat," she said. We both paused for a second and looked at each other, not believing our ears. Tara had just turned two.

Later that same day, I saw a television documentary about the lengths that people are going to look and feel young. The program profiled patients and their doctors who indulge in and perform different forms of plastic surgery or treatments, from botox to liposuction.

These two events had a dramatic effect on me. First, I was genuinely upset with myself because I had to take full responsibility for Tara's "fat" comment. I must ask Sumant on a daily basis if I look fat, and my daughter had obviously picked up on it from me. Although I knew that Tara was always listening to what we said, her comment was a hard lesson in that she is not only listening, but she is also processing and building her self-image by what she sees and hears. I made an instant promise to myself that I would be cognizant about what I said in front of her and that I would make sure that I supported a self-image, for her and for me, that we were beautiful.

The documentary had another effect on me because while I was shocked by the lengths to which people are going to look better and younger, I could also relate to the insecurities that one could have about his or her looks. Aside from feeling "fat," I have always felt insecure about my big nose. Since I was 16 years old, I have debated having a nose job, but I have always found one excuse after another for delaying it. Also, given that I have a father, brother, and husband who are opposed to plastic surgery, it has always been an uphill battle for me. Nonetheless, the timing of the documentary combined with Tara's comment made me think hard about my self-image and how I am influencing my daughter's image of herself.

We live in a society that is obsessed with youth, beauty, and all things physical, but there are so many people who look young and beautiful, yet who are utterly lonely and miserable. I want to find a way to teach my children to feel proud of who they are and what they can achieve, and not judge themselves by how they look. I want them to feel healthy, vibrant, and energetic and to exude beauty because they are happy. I want to support them when they feel down about their looks, but more importantly, I want to show them that inner beauty will always radiate to the outer world.

One small lesson that I took from that day was that the first step in fulfilling my promise to my children is to feel beautiful and happy with myself. As a friend once said to me, I should appreciate my nose because it gives me my look, and for that, I am uniquely beautiful.

The Purple Hat

Age 3: Looks at herself and sees a Queen

Age 8: Looks at herself and sees herself as Cinderella / Sleeping Beauty

Age 15: Looks at herself and sees herself as fat / pimply / ugly (Mom, I can't go to school looking like this!)

Age 20: Looks at herself and sees "too fat / too thin, too short / too tall, too straight / too curly"—but decides she's going anyway.

Age 30: Looks at herself and sees "too fat / too thin, too short / too tall, too straight / too curly"—but decides she doesn't have time so she's going anyway.

Age 40: Looks at herself and sees "too fat / too thin, too short / too tall, too straight / too curly"—but says, "At least, I am clean" and goes anyway.

Age 50: Looks at herself and sees "I am" and goes wherever she wants to go.

Age 60: Looks at herself and reminds herself of all the people who can't even see themselves in the mirror anymore. Goes out and conquers the world.

Age 70: Looks at herself and sees wisdom, laughter, and ability and goes out and enjoys life.

Age 80: Doesn't bother to look. Just puts on a purple hat and goes out to have fun in the world.

Maybe we should all grab that purple hat earlier.

16

I promise to tune in to your feelings and answer your calls for help.

When one of Tara's friends, Ben, became a big brother, it was a difficult time. Ben, just over one-and-a-half years old, was the first child, showered with love and used to the undivided attention of his parents, grandparents, and anyone who was in his little world. When Ben's baby sister, Ruby, was born, his mother was in the hospital for several days, the longest he had ever been away from her, and suddenly everyone was busy gawking over the precious little girl.

The first morning that Ben witnessed his mother breastfeeding was particularly traumatic. He could not understand what was going on. Ben's mother and sister had been home only a day, and his mother seemed so tired from this new baby that had been thrust upon her. But as she held Ruby close to her, Ben's mother looked so tenderly at her, and his father smiled at both of them. Ben watched them with horror and slowly his face began to fall. Ben wasn't able to fully express himself with words, so he did what he had to do to make sure his parents knew how hurt he was.

As tears rolled down his face, Ben ran to his parents' bedroom and grabbed a framed photograph from the bedside table. He stomped back to where his parents sat and showed them the photograph. It was a picture of Ben with his mother and father, all smiling. Ben pointed to himself in the picture and crying hard now said, "Baby! Baby!"

His parents stopped their chatter and looked at little Ben. He was so hurt, calling for attention in the only way that he knew how. His father picked him up and cleared his tears, assuring him that he was still their baby. His mother, finishing Ruby's feed, put the newborn down beside her and gave Ben a big, warm embrace, kissing and patting him in the way that made him feel so warm and comfortable. Ruby squirmed a little, but Ben's mother still sat with him to clear his tears, letting his father pick up his baby sister.

As Ben settled down, his mother told him that she loved him as much as she ever did, if not even more. She told him that things were changing. He was a big brother now, and she was so proud of him. She would need his help with his baby sister, and she knew he could be there for all of them. It was a big task. She promised to try to always listen to him, talk to him as they had talked before, and hug him as they had cuddled before.

Ben settled down, comforted by his mother's voice, and feeling a little bit stronger to deal with the changes ahead.

17

I promise to tell you the many reasons why I am proud of you.

Toilet training provided a new frontier in Tara's development. In many ways, it was an emotional milestone for me, because I had to admit that she was actually growing up and ready to move on to a new stage of development. It was heart-wrenching for me to help her become more independent, even if it was just to go to the potty.

For Tara, it was a major transition. She was at an age where she followed our instructions, but at the same time, it was such an adjustment from her normal routine. Tara knew that we were asking something big of her, and she seemed up to the challenge. We would discuss how all her elder cousins and friends, Mama, Papa, and everyone we knew who was SO big would do *susu* on the toilet. Tara liked the idea of being a big girl like her elder girl cousins.

The first day, Tara thought it was a game to run to the bathroom and wear panties instead of diapers. But by the end of the day, Tara was sick of sitting on her potty chair, and she told me very clearly she did not want to do it anymore. The next morning, when I tried to put a panty on her, Tara was sincerely hurt that I was denying her of her diaper, and she cried until I put the panty away and put the diaper on her. It was so difficult to assess the right way of going through the process because I wanted Tara to feel secure and empowered to make the decision that she was ready to move to this next stage in her life. Manorama, Tara's nanny, and I decided that we would let Tara take the lead in the process and just continue to tell her that she was doing a great job every time she used the potty.

Over the next few days, Tara went through phases in her acceptance and rejection of approaching the toilet. She loved the fact that we all kept telling her how proud we were when she went on the toilet, and she boasted about it on the phone with her grandmothers or to people who visited. When Sumant came home, she ran to give him a hug and say, "Papa, are you proud of me? I did *susu*! Mama is SO proud of me." She was so innocent about the whole thing, knowing that she was doing something that made us happy.

One afternoon, maybe three days after we had started, Manorama took Tara to the toilet. When she took off her diaper, she saw that Tara had already wet it. "Oh, Tara," Manorama gently said, "you already did *susu* in your diaper." Tara beamed back at her, in the most innocent fashion, and replied, "Yes, aren't you SO SO proud of me! I did so much *susu*!" Manorama smiled at Tara's innocence and gave her a hug, telling her that we were all always proud of her.

Tara's comment is a reminder to all of us about the sensitivity and innocence of our young children and how everything we say to them is used to build their sense of self.

18

I promise to trust you to navigate your world.

"Shall I take Tara to the park today?"

It was a simple question, but I felt like I had been struck by lightening. My pulse began to race, my palms were suddenly damp, and I could not think straight. Until that moment, Tara had always been with me, Sumant, one of our parents, or someone in the family whom I completely trusted.

While I trusted Angela, my cleaning woman who played with Tara some days when I had to work at home, I could not be sure that she could secure Tara in her stroller correctly, that she would know when Tara wanted her milk, and that she would sense when Tara was cold and needed her cardigan. There were so many variables involved in going to the park, variables that I felt only I knew how to control for my child.

It took a few seconds to gather my breath, and meekly I replied, "Sure." I took another sigh. "It is a beautiful day, no? I am sure she would love it." Who would have thought these would be some of the most difficult words I would ever say up to that moment in my life? As I packed Tara's diaper bag, I tried to focus on what needed to be inside, rather than on the knots that were twisting inside my stomach.

I walked Tara and Angela to the door, suddenly thinking that I, too, could use a walk and some fresh air, justifying that I could get my work done later. But deep down inside, I knew that it was important to let Tara go to the park that day. It was an important milestone for me.

My cousin told me about the first day she dropped her son off at preschool. She had put on a brave front as he held on to her knees, pleading with her not to leave him there. She told him that he would be okay, that he would love school, and that she would pick him up very soon. As she watched him from outside, she saw that within thirty seconds he was distracted, playing in the sand with a shovel and pail. She went to the car, closed the door, and sobbed her heart out.

I remember the day I left for college. My parents dropped me off, and when I called several hours later to see if they had reached home, my dad made up an excuse about why my mother could not come to the phone. I knew she was too emotional to speak. Four years later when Gotham left for college, it took more than a week for my mother not to break down into tears when his name was mentioned.

Years later, I was moving to India to get married. I left the United States about a month before the wedding. My mother was already in India, and Gotham and my father were to travel there for the wedding two weeks later. I will never forget my last day at home in my parents' house. I was so consumed with packing and making my final calls that I realized only when my father and I sat in the car to go to the airport that he had been avoiding me all day. He sat in silence in the car, and suddenly it dawned on me that I was leaving. I remember turning back to wave goodbye as I boarded the plane, his back to me, his hands obviously wiping away a reservoir of tears.

Tara and Angela returned from the park about ar hour and a half later. As I heard the front door open, I ran to my desk, pretending that I had been working, not frantically pacing. I casually turned to them as Angela pushed the stroller into the apartment. Tara was soundly asleep in her stroller, strapped in perfectly with her cardigan on and a peaceful smile on her face.

SEED SILENCE

By Harry Alfred Wiggett

I did not hear you fall
From pod to mother earth.
I did not hear you call
Or cry your humble birth.
I did not hear you sigh
As silently you grew.
I did not hear a Why
Because God made you you.
And yet your silence spoke
Of confidence and might
And purpose as you broke
Through earth into the light.

19

I promise to reach for balance
in my life and yours.

One of my biggest challenges as a mother has been to figure out the balance between my professional ambitions and giving my children everything I want to give them in terms of time, attention, and participation. I see this challenge mirrored in most of my friends who are mothers, as well as amongst most professional women whom I know or admire. How do I forge ahead in my career while being the mother I want to be?

So many of my friends—MDs, MBAs, PhDs, advertising executives, producers, and consultants—have spent years studying and working to achieve professional success. But with motherhood, many have given up work to stay at home with their babies. They do not see it as a sacrifice, but rather as something they want to do, a precious time in their lives that will never come again. But it is also very hard on many of them. Being at home is difficult for a mind that is racing with ideas and used to the melodrama, intellectualism, and social interactions of the workplace. It is a big change and one that leaves many truly unhappy.

I know other women who knew early on they would not be happy at home or could not afford to leave the workplace and returned to work after maternity leave.

Many of them are plagued with pangs of guilt or questioning if they are doing the right thing.

After two children, I have to admit that I still struggle at times to find the balance between my projects and feeling that I have not given enough time to my children. I continually reassess what I am doing and have evolved to forgive myself for achieving less at work to spend more time with my babies. But I have also realized that I will be the best mother I can be when I am happy, fulfilled, and confident. And honestly, I am all those things when I can be both a mom and a professional of some sorts. Most important, I have realized that, for me, being a good mother is not quantified by the time, activities, or tasks I achieve with my children.

Motherhood is not about to-do lists, projects accomplished, grades, promotions, titles, or tasks. Motherhood is about loving, caring, listening, and holding. It is about nurturing your children, watching them blossom, guiding them, and cherishing every precious moment that they are cuddled in your arms, giggling with you, and sharing their discoveries. It is about truly being with them in body, mind, and spirit. It is about being happy with who you are as a person, so that they, too, can shine with pride, accomplishment, and security.

20

I promise to show you that together we can create a better world.

I was five months pregnant on September 11th.

That morning, Sumant and I were still asleep when the phone rang. My father was hysterical on the line. His plane had just landed in Chicago, and the news was flashing on the overhead screens in the airport. Minutes before my father's plane had landed, the first plane had crashed into the North Tower. At first, we could not really understand what he was saying, but as we rushed to turn on the television, the nightmare began to dawn on us.

My father remained frantic. My brother, Gotham, had just boarded an American Airlines plane from New York to Los Angeles. The first reports on the news were that they thought that the plane that crashed into the first tower was an American Airlines plane that had left JFK for LA at nine A.M. That would be Gotham's flight.

As we were on the phone with my father, the confused broadcasters kept getting updated information. I tried to calm my father down as Sumant got more news. My aunt called on the other line. Hearing the same initial reports about the flight, she had already tracked down the car company that had driven Gotham to the airport and was getting the specifics on his flight.

And then the second plane crashed into the South tower. We watched in horror, unable to comprehend what was going on. At that moment, the panic really began to set in. We still could not track down Gotham. My mother was on a flight from London to New York. My cousin, Kanika, worked close to that area in New York City. Names of friends and people who worked in the World Trade Center came racing to mind. It was so overwhelming that we did not know what to do. We were totally powerless as the horrific news and images continued to broadcast before us.

The next few hours were a blur. First the news that the flights were from Boston confirmed that Gotham was not on one of the planes that had crashed, but it took about five hours before we heard from him. In that time, the other two flights went down and no one knew what would happen next. It would be another nine hours before my mother's plane landed. Our calls to British Airways revealed that her plane had turned around two hours before landing in New York and headed back to London. My aunt called to say that Kanika was okay and had walked home from downtown to the Upper West Side. She was with a friend whose husband was on the fiftieth floor of one of the buildings. They were praying, anxiously waiting to hear from him.

We all have our memories and nightmares of 9/11. For me, it took two days for the panic to subside—to track down my friends and family, to connect with people, to just get my breath again, and to turn the television off.

Two days after 9/11, I was going for a walk, and I fainted. The stress combined with the pregnancy forced my body to stop for a minute. I spent the next two days in the hospital where I avoided television and focused again on the baby growing inside of me and thought about her future and the world that I was bringing her into. How was I going to protect my unborn child from the violence and hatred in this world? Where could we escape from the horror, hatred, fear, and sadness that had consumed the past forty-eight hours?

In the midst of my personal fear, a more fundamental discomfort started to take over. How could I deny that others had suffered and were suffering, and only now, when faced with violence in my own land and vulnerability in my own family, did I truly panic? What about the millions of innocent people and children who had been slaughtered years earlier in Rwanda; the daily killings in the name of religion in Israel and Palestine; the ravages of disease, poverty, and hunger that accosted the streets of India, Africa, and even the inner cities of the United States? What about the terrorist acts that took place daily in India, Pakistan, Serbia, Colombia, Afghanistan, and East Timor?

I began to question every thought, feeling, and emotion I had. The world was being depicted in black and white, the bravado of "You're With US or Against US" and Good versus Evil. It was a sentiment that I could not understand. The terrorists also had families, mothers who loved them, brothers and sisters, dreams, hopes, and ambitions. What drove them to such an act of terror? What was creating such hatred and conviction in these individuals? What did their mothers think when they saw them hurt themselves and others in such a violent act? What was my role in this drama of an eye for an eye, retaliation, and the search for justice?

I am still struggling with these questions, and I watch with a sinking heart as revenge and war cloud world politics. In the context of raising a child, however, the issues have become all the more relevant and urgent for me. I now truly have a responsibility that goes beyond my own small sphere of relationships and daily activities.

As parents, we are bringing a new generation of children into this world. We are shaping their values, priorities, concerns, and feelings. We have the responsibility to teach them about love, kindness, and empathy. From us they learn about understanding, tolerance, sympathy, and compassion.

We have taken on the most important roles of our lifetimes—shaping the global citizens of tomorrow. These citizens will face hardship, violence, and conflict, but hopefully they will also bring some light, hope, and inspiration to those around them. Our role in creating some peace and justice in the future starts at home, by influencing our children to have love and compassion for those around them. This is a mandate that can inspire us with a sense of hope and purpose that we have never glimpsed before.

Reflection

WHAT DO YOU WANT to teach your child about other cultures, religions, and ways of thinking? What type of world do you want to show him or her?

Traditions

Rituals and history I want to share

(and create) with you

21

I promise to celebrate each milestone in your life.

I get excited and emotional thinking about all the special times that we can look forward to in our lives together. There is so much to plan for your future, so much I want to share and experience with you, and already I am nostalgic that these good times will pass too soon.

I imagine preparing for the new school year, planning your clothes and school supplies and choosing your lunch box and backpack. I think about your graduations from preschool to college. I feel the pride welling in my chest as I see all that you have learned and accomplished over the years. I sense the overwhelming emotions year after year, realizing that you are growing up.

I think about dance and music recitals, celebrating sports victories, and consoling your little heart after defeats. I wonder what special interests and talents you will develop, and I eagerly anticipate learning about these new hobbies with you.

I think about what it will be like to teach you to drive a car. What a step it will be to give you the reins to your own freedom and to let you wander by yourself. I think about letting you go on your first trip alone or with friends, wanting to give you all the resources to be comfortable and safe, but knowing that it is time to let you discover the world on your own.

I imagine my heart skipping a beat when you tell me that you have fallen in love. How protective will I be, not wanting you to ever get hurt? I think about how we will tell your father, knowing that he will immediately want to shield you and that I will have to hold him back, even though I want to do the same.

And I think about what it will be like to watch you, my most precious baby, grown up, independent, and conquering the world. I will still see you as my baby, soft and safe in my arms, amazed at all that you have become. I know I will have to hold back the tears of memory and pride and the nostalgia of all that we have done together during this wonderful journey.

22

I promise to give you gifts that build your character, values, and spirit.

Around the world, mothers collect special objects for their daughters that they will give to them when they get married. In India, a new mother often begins collecting jewelry and saris for her daughter, even before she is born. In the American tradition, mothers put special objects in hope chests that are passed on to their daughters when they get married. The hope chest becomes a symbol of all the hope and love that parents hold for their daughters and their future. Traditionally, hope chests have been filled with linens, fabrics, quilts, china, and all the things that would help to make a daughter a good wife.

Creating hope chests for my daughters is one of those special, meaningful, and emotional journeys that I will make as a mother. It will take years to find physical objects that represent the hopes, dreams, love, and pride that I envision for them. It is a journey that will take time and thought, and heartfelt diligence.

I want to fill their hope chests with optimism, empowerment, freedom, curiosity, adventure, peace, spirituality, and unbounded energy. I want to give them great stories, art that I have collected, philosophy from great thinkers, poetry from the ages, tickets to explore the corners of the earth, mantras to delve into their souls, recipes to nurture their bodies, and heirlooms to remember their family and those who were here before them. I want to write their stories from childhood, about visits to the zoo and trips to foreign lands. I want to collect the pictures that they draw over the years and make collages of photographs of our special times together. I want to give them treasures that will make them conscious human beings who care for and love the earth and those around them.

I want their hope chests to represent our love and the bonds that we share. I want them to be able to dip into their hope chests to find new treasures at different times in their lives, when they are happy and sad, confident, or in need of a helping hand. And through these gifts, I want my daughters to know that they are my most beloved gifts in this world.

23

I promise to support you as you take on new endeavors.

One of the most special times in my life was the month after I had Tara. Discovering my little baby girl was like watching a miracle blossom in front of my eyes. She was the most precious, beautiful, and divine being I had ever laid my eyes on.

But there was another aspect of this time that I will also treasure forever. In the tradition that is followed by many Indians, a new mother and her infant move back to their family home for forty days after birth. The tradition recognizes the fact that both mother and child need nurturing and caring in those first weeks. The new mother, by being taken care of by her own mother, can focus on the challenges and discoveries of her baby and begin their journey together in a stable environment.

Returning home with my newborn was a very emotional and touching experience. While I go home all the time, entering my parents' house in this new phase of my life, with my own child in my arms, was a beautiful and moving moment. I was an adult now, expanding our family and stirring up emotions of unbounded love. I could see the love and pride in my parents' eyes for both me and their granddaughter, and I realized that just as Tara was a gift for Sumant and me, she was also the most sacred gift they had ever received.

Over the next few weeks, I bonded with my mother in a way that we had never bonded before. Her wisdom, her ability to take care of me and my baby, and her tireless compassion and care for Tara and me left me speechless and in total awe. In the middle of the night, if Tara continued to fidget after her feeding, my mother was at our side, quietly taking care of both of us. In her gentle manner, my mother gave Sumant and I the space we needed as new parents, but she took away much of the overwhelming fear that also gripped us in this new phase of our life. Nani, my grandmother, was with each of her daughters each time they had a child. It was her role as a mother to care for her children, and now my mother was doing the same.

In contrast to my experience, I had a friend who had a baby at the same time as me. She was a single mother who did not have a close relationship with her mother. She told me about her struggle to manage on her own, relying on friends and extended family in those few weeks. Yet when I told her about my story and this new bond I was developing with my mother, she softened, her voice full of hope as she told me how exciting it would be for us one day when we could care for our children's children.

Those initial moments of love for our newborn babies are just the first glimpses into the lifelong opportunities that we have to grow and bond with them.

24

I promise to help you discover your unique place in a modern world.

A Pakistani American friend of mine traveled back to Karachi to visit her grandparents and extended family. While she had been born in the United States, she had grown up in a strong Pakistani community where she learned Urdu, ate traditional food, celebrated all the holidays, and identified herself as being Pakistani, as well as American. In fact, it was her South Asian and Muslim heritage that gave her a sense of self, identity, culture, and context. My friend had always felt somewhat different in the United States when she was not among her own community. She anticipated the feeling of security, belonging, and homecoming as she walked off the plane in Karachi.

However, it was far from the homecoming she had imagined. In many ways, my friend felt like a fish out of water—she stood out even more in Karachi than in the United States. Even though she tried to assimilate by wearing outfits similar to her cousins and by not speaking much in public so her accent wouldn't give her away, she found that the locals could tell she was a foreigner from miles away. Perhaps it was her walk, her posture, or even just the way she breathed. Even her cousins and relatives treated her a bit differently, explaining things to her more slowly. They would often refer to her as the "American" cousin when talking to others, or assume that she did not understand a conversation that they were having. My friend was sad to admit that many times they were right; she did not fit in the same way. She was a foreigner in this land, as well.

One evening, her grandfather asked her if she would like to see a family tree that had been passed on for generations. She could barely sit still as he slid aside a painting that covered a safe, which he carefully unlocked. He took out an old piece of parchment that was rolled up. He laid the parchment on a table, put on his reading glasses, and slowly began to spread it out.

"This, my dear, is our family tree. My great-grandfather passed it on to my father, who passed it on to me. I would like to show it to you."

As my friend looked at the ancient parchment, she gasped with awe. The family tree went back over numerous centuries. "Yes, my dear. This family tree shows how we are direct descendants of Mohammad. We have a very great and important role in this world to fulfill." Her grandfather now pointed slowly to his name on the piece of paper. "Here I am, with my brothers. Here is your father, and here is your brother. And here is my father, his father, and the generations of our ancestors before us."

My friend sat silently, her eyes slowly filling up with tears, as her grandfather proudly followed the lineage up. There were no women on the parchment, except for one. It amazed her as she looked upon the name—it was Fatima, the only child and daughter of Mohammed. Because of her, the rest of the lineage existed, yet still no other woman was mentioned.

"But, Grandfather," she politely stopped him in mid-sentence. "Where I am I on this family tree? Where is my mother? My aunts and grandmothers?" He blinked in response. The woman realized in that instant that he had never even thought about it. No one had ever asked such a question before.

He silently gestured to his granddaughter to give him a pen, and in front of her, he wrote her name next to her brothers. Then he continued to fill in the names of other women in her family. My friend's heart pounded with excitement as she watched history, her history, being corrected. Soon, her grandmother and several cousins were peering over her shoulder, watching him correct the family tree. There was a silent emotion in the room that could not be expressed in words.

Later, my friend overheard her grandmother gossiping with her friends as they played cards. She heard oohs and aahs and could not resist entering the parlor in which they played. As she walked in, one of her grandmother's friends looked at her and asked her grandmother in Urdu, "Is this the American daughter you speak of?" Her grandmother smiled proudly and nodded. "Well done," the woman nodded to her, and the others gazed at her adoringly. "In America, they teach you to speak, no? Well done, my dear, well done."

My friend smiled back and confidently replied in Urdu, "Thank you."

Reflection

DRAW A FAMILY TREE for your child. Include the city, state, or country from which each family member came.

25

I promise to share the myths and history of our culture.

There is a series of comic books in India, called Amar Chitra Kathas, which illustrate stories from classic Indian mythology. These comic books are pretty amazing because they distill not only the complicated tales, but also the lessons and values from these great texts. When my brother, Gotham, and I were young, we used to love reading these comic books. In fact, Gotham was somewhat obsessed with them, and so our parents would collect them for him during our many trips to India. Because of these comics, we were familiar with Indian mythology at a young age.

Since Tara was 6 months old, she and Sumant have had a ritual while going to sleep. It is a time that they both relish—talking, cuddling, reading books, and catching up on the day. I generally do not join them during their nightly ritual because it is some rare quiet time that I get to myself.

One night, however, I decided to go to bed early, and I rested as Tara and Sumant began their nightly ritual. Tara had just turned two, and at this point, she and Sumant had two-way conversations about their days. Tara would tell her father exactly what she wanted or didn't want to do (drink water, not milk; sleep with the yellow blanket, not the brown one; hold her big pig, not the small one). But, I noticed that this night, instead of reading one of her favorite books—*Curious George* or *Caps for Sale* or *The Cat in the Hat*—Tara casually reached under the bed, pulled out an Amar Chitra Katha comic book, jumped into Sumant's lap, and began turning the pages. As they sat together, Sumant would point out a character, such as the Indian God, Krishna, and then tell Tara about him. Tara would then repeat his name and ask, "Papa, what's Krishna doing?" And Sumant would begin to tell her in the most basic language the words that Krishna was reciting to Arjun in the Mahabharata (one of India's greatest texts).

As they turned the pages, I saw how engrossed Tara was in hearing her father tell the tales of this great mythology. She would then show Sumant her muscles and say, "Papa, look, Tara is as strong as Krishna." Towards the end of the comic, there was a picture of Krishna's mother doing a prayer, and my eyes filled with tears as Tara began to sing one of the traditional prayers out loud as she clasped her hands together.

I smiled and watched Sumant and Tara kiss each other and lie down to sleep. They then began to say good night to everyone in her world. "Good night, Mama. Good night, Papa. Good night, Gotham Mamo. Good night, Candi Mami. Good night, Cleo. Good night, Dadi. Good night, Dada, Good night, Nani. Good night, Nana. Good night, Chachu. Good night, Krishna. Good night, Arjun. Good night, Bhagvanji (God)." Tara closed her eyes and with a small smile on her face, she entered a world of dreams filled with family, friends, gods, and goddesses who loved her.

Tara has shown me that mythology, parables, and ancient tales resonate with color, passion, adventure, and deeply rooted lessons. Sharing these tales with our children gives them a glimpse into magical, spiritual, and powerful legends that can help nurture and ignite their imaginations.

26

I promise to practice traditions that will feed you for a lifetime.

"Bhabhiji, why do you always set aside a portion of food at dinner?" It was a tradition she had always kept.

Bhabhiji, my great-grandmother, stared beyond the slowly spinning fan above, her voice barely audible at first as she reeled in images from another world. A frail figure, lost in a sheer white sari, she sat on a hard bed, several pillows supporting her worn body. A stagnant room, white plastered walls, incense teasing a tattered picture of her husband, Rudraksha beads wrapped around her finger. Shooting fleeting glances in our direction just long enough to make sure we understood the words she wanted us to hear, Bhabhiji told us a story that has been passed down through our family for generations.

It's a story of a young boy. He must have been six or seven years old at the time. They said he had the clearest of faces—innocent and joyful with the kind of clearness that a sage remembers when he attains enlightenment, and deep, dark eyes of a shimmering black that twinkled like lone stars brightening up an infinite universe.

Seven generations ago, there was a war in northwest India with massive killings, bloody tortures, and innocent victims. It was one of those turbulent and violent times that are common throughout history, with one group of people being perse-cuted by another because of religion. Our family had seen loved ones dragged from their homes and beaten alive—savage realities that are too horrible to imagine.

Our family members, too, were in danger. In an effort to save their children, they decided to leave their home and flee deeper into India where such persecution did not exist. It was a perilous journey; if they were caught, they undoubtedly would be killed. They left with neither money nor possessions, only their seven sons and the desire to survive.

It was a rainy night, full of thunder, crying winds, and wandering spirits. They left their home, perhaps on foot, perhaps in a cart. They traveled for hours. They heard from other refugees that it was a risky night; others had been discovered and killed for trying to escape.

Eventually they came to a river. To continue, they had to find some way to cross it. They found a boatman. He was an older man, pale and somber, with an empty and desolate expression. He had a good-sized boat that could take them across the river.

The boatman eyed this family approaching him to save their lives. He saw a family with seven sons—a family committed to one another. He saw the fear in their eyes, but more than that he felt the love that emanated from their souls. He envied the feeling they had for each other. He once had a wife and a child, but both were dead now. The boatman was all alone, and this unbearable loneliness was slowly killing him.

Of course, our family did not know the boatman's desperation. They begged him to take them across the river. They had no money and could think of no way to repay him. The old man eyed the children. In an attempt to save himself, he asked for one of the sons as payment.

At first, our family was horrified. To give away a son was to lose a part of themselves. War, however, brings new insights to people. Our family could see the pain and suffering in the old man's eyes. They feared for their own lives because they had so much to live for, but a more insidious and calculating death preyed upon this man. He had nothing to hope for, nothing to live for. In a moment of desperation, compassion, and salvation, our family agreed to give their youngest son to this man to save the lives of their children and to save the boatman's life as well.

And so the story has been told for seven generations, and our family began a tradition that Bhabhiji continued to follow throughout her lifetime. During every meal, one plate of food was set aside for the little boy who was left behind. When everyone was done with their meal, the plate was given to a poor child who lived in the streets outside.

As Bhabhiji finished her story, she was silent for a few moments, lost in her reverie. Then she quietly said, "Perhaps it is a silly tradition that an old woman holds on to. But such traditions keep us connected, no? They help us to remember and to cherish what we have."

With that, she slowly filled up a plate and set it aside. She closed her eyes in prayer, and we all thanked the little boy who had saved the lives of his family and a lonely old man.

27

I promise to celebrate holidays with you that will help us to connect with each other and the world.

Thanksgiving in our household had its own spicy twist.

As Indians who had immigrated to the United States, the whole concept of turkeys, pilgrims, football, apple pie, and Native Americans with feathers in their hair seemed quite foreign to my parents.

But over time, the day began to hold a lot of meaning and significance. It represented a time to recognize all that they could be grateful for—health, family, success, and happiness. My parents and many of our relatives welcomed family members who would come to Boston from around the country for the gathering. A huge feast was planned for the day, including masala turkey, spicy Indian vegetable filling, and traditional Indian potatoes on the side. Dessert was a combination of apple pies, brownies, and traditional Indian desserts. Bollywood music played in the background, while my brother and other cousins dragged our elders to the television and tried to explain the game of football to them. After genuinely trying to understand the game for a few minutes, the elders would quickly lose interest and drift outside to play cricket.

My memories of Thanksgiving mark an important lesson in how I want to celebrate holidays with my children. We live in a multicultural society where we marry people of other cultures, from different backgrounds, with different ideologies and religious beliefs. Our holidays and customs build the foundation for how we identify ourselves and to whom we are connected. While Sumant identifies himself as Indian, I identify myself as an Indian American. How will my children identify themselves? Is there a need for them to identify themselves in our multicultural society?

I have struggled with whether or not to get a Christmas tree. We are not Christian, so why would we celebrate the holiday? (When we were young, my parents would buy us one gift each and hang up a stocking by the fireplace. Christmas was not about gifts, but it became a day we learned about giving.) At the same time, I do not want my young children to feel excluded from the dominant society. I want them to know about Indian festivals like Diwali (the festival of light that marks the New Year) and Holi (the festival of color). But I also want them to understand the traditions and holidays of their friends—from Ramadan and Id to Hanukah and the Chinese Moon Festival.

In a world of so much color and flavor, perhaps the answer is to create a calendar of holidays that we celebrate throughout the year. This calendar is full of rich traditions, color, stories, and most of all connections—bonds with your heritage, world, self, and the friends and families you love.

Reflection

THINK ABOUT HOW you would like to celebrate holidays with your children. What are the lessons you would like them to learn from these important times?

28

I promise to give you the confidence to create new ways of doing old things.

My father was the eldest brother in his extended family. This position alone garnered him respect from all of his younger cousins. Also, because my grandfather served as an anchor for his family and the community in general, his wife and children were extended respect by their relationship to him.

As is traditional in India, my father was called "Deepak Bhaya," bhaya being the deferential term of respect given to an elder brother. He was always given the first plate of food and the first choice of presents. But there was one tradition that made my father uncomfortable. My grandmother's brother, who was an admiral in the Indian navy, believed very strongly in hierarchy, the order of things, and tradition. He had two sons, Amit and Bharat, with whom he was very strict. Both boys were extraordinarily bright, talented, well-behaved, and the darlings of the whole family. Their father would present them, always well-coiffed, hair and uniforms in place, singing songs to entertain the other members of the family.

When Amit and Bharat were young, maybe three and four respectively, they came to Delhi to visit my grandmother and her family. Upon seeing my father, they were instructed by my uncle to touch my father's feet because he was their elder brother. Touching another's feet in India is a symbolic gesture of deference and respect. My father, albeit fifteen years older than the young boys, was not comfortable with this gesture, but he was in his late teens and was too fearful of his domineering uncle to protest, so he awkwardly responded to the young boys by touching their heads in recognition.

Years passed, with my parents moving to the United States, and my father garnering more courage to speak his mind. When Bharat came to Boston to attend Harvard College, it had been years since my father had seen Amit and Bharat. I remember going to the airport with my father to pick up Bharat. As soon as Bharat saw my father, he automatically bent down to touch my father's feet. My father looked so awkward that he immediately responded by bending down and touching Bharat's feet in return! The expression on Bharat's face was priceless. It was almost as if my father had shattered his worldview, and he did not know how to respond. So Bharat touched my father's feet again, and in turn, my dad once again returned the gesture. Finally, my father stopped Bharat and gave him a welcoming embrace.

Recently, I was at a family event when two young cousins, probably seven and nine years old, arrived. As was the custom, they went around the room touching all the elders' feet. When they bent down to touch Bharat's feet, Bharat immediately held them back and returned the gesture to the young kids. The elders in the room raised their eyebrows in surprise, and Bharat's father looked on in shock. The boys bent down again, and so did Bharat, laughing as he watched them try to come to terms with this new tradition.

As I watched this episode, I could not help but think about how important it is to respect old traditions, but also to always question and adapt them. We cannot just tell our children to do something because it has been done before. We owe them the thoughtful explanations that will give them respect for age-old ways, and if those reasons don't make sense anymore, we must be willing to let the traditions go.

Reflection

WRITE A PROMISE to your child about following (or not following) a certain family tradition and explain why this is important to you.

29

I promise to show you the power that comes from small rituals.

Every evening after their dinner, my aunt and uncle, Saroj Bainji and Pal Uncle, share a grapefruit. It has been a tradition they have kept for more than forty years of marriage. The dirty plates and cutlery are put in the sink, and the remaining dinner is put on a counter to be packed later.

Saroj Bainji picks a ripe grapefruit from the ever-present, carefully-chosen selection in the fruit basket. If a guest or several guests are over for dinner, the appropriate number of extra grapefruits are also brought to the table. Saroj Bainji brings her favorite knife, sits comfortably back in her chair, and begins to peel the juicy fruit while Pal Uncle gets comfortable.

As Saroj Bainji peels, they discuss the evening conversation with the grandchildren, the latest family problems that need to be addressed, a challenging or intriguing patient, or the state of the world in general. On some days, there may not be much to talk about or they may be tired, and they'll sit in relative silence, not necessarily needing words to complete the ritual. Saroj Bainji eats half the fruit, and Pal Uncle eats the other half.

Day after day, month after month, for years on end, they have shared their evening grapefruit in this manner. It is the most relaxing time of their day, a half hour that after so many years is almost taken for granted, but this is nonetheless one of the most important moments in their daily lives. Even on those days when they have had a disagreement, the grapefruit is shared, often serving as the impetus for breaking down those angry barriers that are so easy to build.

For Saroj Bainji and Pal Uncle, the grapefruit has come to represent that time at the end of every day when they connect with each other. It is a time when they both can breathe, when they can process the day's events, and when they can check in to make sure that the other one is doing well. Through the grapefruit, they know when life is in balance, when their relationship is in balance, and when it is time to once again connect with themselves or each other. It is a small, conscious time, every day, during which they commit once again to their love for each other and their need to communicate, to share, and to be there for one another.

Such small rituals provide the context for connection in our lives. Attention to the precious moments that we sometimes take for granted can help us to find magical ways to create lasting bonds with those we love.

30

I promise to help you to retrace the footsteps of your ancestors.

In the Hindu tradition in India, when someone dies they are cremated and their ashes are taken to the holy river, the Ganges. Normally, the offspring of the deceased will make a pilgrimage to Varanasi, a holy city, to scatter and release the ashes in the flowing waters.

When my grandfather died several years ago, my father, my uncle and his wife, and my grandmother's brothers made the pilgrimage to Varanasi to complete the final rites. It was an extremely emotional time, and each one had their own ghosts, happy and sad memories, hopes, and disappointments that accompanied them on the journey.

As they stood on the steps by the bank of the river that evening, they lit traditional lamps and said a prayer before sprinkling my grandfather's ashes into the water. They watched the moonlight and the glow from the lamps illuminate what was now only dust as it flowed away from them, free forever.

They were getting ready to depart when two holy men approached them. The men were dressed in traditional saffron robes, and they were barefoot with black ash spread along their bodies. Their foreheads were marked with the traditional red tikkas that indicated long hours of meditation and prayer. In their hands, the holy men each carried a pile of tattered pamphlets, pieces of paper scrawled with notes in indecipherable handwriting.

The holy men asked my father the name of the deceased and his place of birth, birth date, and the name of his father. My father, intrigued, answered all of the questions and stood by as the two men consulted each other and the piles of tattered paper. After about ten minutes, they said they had found the file.

The holy men showed my family a recording, written by my grandfather, Daddy, when he had been there more than fifty years earlier, performing the last rites for his father. He had listed his brothers who had made the journey with him. Before Daddy's entry, there was an entry by his father. He had been to this same spot three times in his lifetime, once when his father had died, once right after he had been married, and again when Daddy was a toddler. In his last entry, he had written, in neat English, about how Daddy was being mischievous during their trip, but that he was awed by his son's beauty. He said that Daddy looked like the great Indian poet, Rabindranath Tagore, when he was a baby and so he had nicknamed him Togo. My father and uncle could not hold back the tears because they knew now why they had both always loved the poet's work.

My father then asked the holy men how far back the records went. They returned to their papers and soon pulled out an entry written by my father's great-grandfather. This time it was written in Urdu and again referred to the last rites of releasing his father's ashes. They had pages and pages of records, all linked to our family, each telling similar stories. Some simply listed names, places, and professions, while others told stories of love and war, hopes and dreams. The entries dated back to before Christ, back to 300 BC, the time of Alexander the Great.

Then the holy men told their fascinated audience that it was time to update the files. They took out a broken pencil and wrote down the names of my father, uncle, aunt, and grandmother's brothers. They asked for their wives and children's names and completed the family tree through the current generation, listing my three cousins, my brother, myself, and my husband, Sumant. The men gave my family the opportunity to share any thoughts or feelings with future generations. Then, with a simple bow, the two holy men departed.

When my father returned to Delhi and called us in the United States to tell us about his pilgrimage, we noted that the journey had helped to release his desperate sorrow. As he told us the story about the two holy men, we understood the realization that he had about the cycle of life and death. While it was a sad time for all of us, we could also see that Daddy's existence, like all of ours, was part of the natural rhythm of the universe. There was comfort in the knowledge that while our souls come and go, there is a bond with those who were there before us.

My father had felt a connection to those who had made the same journey as he had, telling us with hope and excitement about the secrets he had left for Gotham and me, for his grandchildren, and for the generations that were yet to come. And in making that journey, my father had found some solace, hope, and happiness in the knowledge that even when he is gone, there will be a record that he had loved and connected with a lineage that was bigger than just him.

Generations come and go like breezes in the wind,
The fragrance of your ancestors lingers here.
From the keeper of our family records in Varanasi

Choices

How you shape your destiny

31

I promise to create a loving and enriching environment for you.

As a mother, I am always thinking about the environment that my babies are growing up in. I think about how their perceptions of the world are influenced by what they hear, see, smell, taste, touch, and experience. I think about how their senses of self will be nurtured by feeling love and peace in their lives. There is a well-known story from Chinese philosophy about the mother of Mencius, one of Confucius's most famous disciples, and the choices she made when bringing up her son.

When Mencius was a child, his family lived near a cemetery. One day, his mother observed that Mencius and his young friends were pretending to be in a funeral procession and were staging the last rites for each other. This was not the environment in which she wanted to raise her son, so she decided to move. This was not an easy task in 300 BC.

They moved near a market. Soon enough, Mencius's mother observed her son haggling with his friends and gloating when he was able to trick one of his comrades to win a play negotiation. She realized that these were not the values that she wanted to teach her son, so she packed their bags once again and moved to a small hut that lay on the perimeter of a school. Now she observed her son enviously watching the other children read books, discuss science and philosophy, and be courteous to their elders and fellow students. Mencius began to imitate their behavior, and he became one of the greatest thinkers and philosophers of his time.

32

I promise to help you look for the hidden meaning behind events.

When I was twenty-three, I moved to India to help launch MTV Asia. I wanted to live in India so that I could spend time with my grandparents and get to know the country where I had been born but had never lived. I never anticipated that the purpose of my trip was to meet my husband, my partner in life and the father of my babies.

On my first day in New Delhi, my cousin invited me to her house for a party. Her house was famous in Delhi for its parties, and this particular one was dubbed a "graffiti party." Everyone wore white clothes and was given a pack of colorful, washable markers. The markers were used to draw pictures or write funny messages, insights, and flirtations on the clothes of other party members. It was a lighthearted, fun, and amusing evening. As the new girl in town, I was surrounded by new friends, and my white shirt quickly became a mosaic of color, words, and innovative pictures.

There was one person who stood out that night. He was a tall, slender, athletic man with a beautiful smile, a casual gait, and a relaxed, friendly manner. He had approached me after hearing from his friends about the new girl with a cool tattoo on her back. We spoke for only a minute or two, and I could not even remember his name by the end of the night. However, I left the party with an enchanted feeling and the notion that somehow my life was going to change because of this short interaction with this new person.

I returned home, gave my t-shirt to the servant to be washed, and slept soundly that evening. The next morning, my shirt came back from the laundry, bright white with all the color, drawings, and words gone, except for one patch right by my heart. On it, in blue marker, was written "Sumant" with a phone number beneath it. Immediately, I knew that this was the man I had met the evening before, and that my life was changed forever. I picked up the phone and called Sumant, and after one dinner I knew that I was going to spend the rest of my life with him. We were married a year and a half later.

I learned later that one of Sumant's friends had told him to approach me, and Sumant responded by saying, "If I do, I will be stuck for life." And he quickly picked up a new marker, one that was permanent and not erasable, approached me, wrote on my shirt, and left immediately. My shirt was the only one he wrote on that evening.

At every turn in life, there are interactions, moments, relationships, and situations that have tremendous meaning and power. The fun is interpreting the messages, unraveling the hints, and taking advantage of opportunities to create what you want. When something makes you stop for a moment, pay attention. There may be a whole new world of magic that is just waiting to unfold.

Reflection

THINK ABOUT A CHANCE encounter that had significant consequences for you and your baby's life.

33

I promise to show you the freedom that comes from being able to laugh at yourself.

Tara has taught Sumant and me that we cannot control everything around us and that some of those things that we thought were so important or serious are really not. She has taught us about freedom—freedom from being self-conscious, freedom from worrying about what others think, and freedom to smile and laugh at ourselves with abandon.

I remember several weeks after Tara was born, Sumant and I were going out together for our first dinner alone while my mother watched her. I had gotten my hair cut, put on makeup, took out a new shirt, and finally felt fresh and alive. I reached down to pick Tara up and give her a hug, and, of course, she spat up on me. We were late already, and I had to admit it was the perfect ending to a night of preening! Even now, every time I wear a new or nice shirt, it inevitably ends up "decorated" with spaghetti sauce or smeared peas. Such stains are the badges of honor of motherhood.

Sumant and I were at a fancy restaurant another night, celebrating a friend's promotion. Tara, of course, did a big potty the minute we sat down. In the bathroom, there was no changing table, but rather a long line of women in fancy clothes dabbing their faces before the crowded mirror. As I struggled to change Tara's diaper while standing in a corner, I suddenly felt something smelly smear across my face. I could only laugh as the crowd of women quickly dispersed to give me room at the sink.

Another time, when we were at a café for a cup of coffee, Tara sang nursery rhymes at the top of her lungs. She was not self-conscious, but instead reveled in hearing her beautiful voice. As a woman wearing a skimpy outfit entered the café, everyone gave her side glances, but Tara yelled at the top of her lungs, "Mama, look at her tummy!"

On a day where my complexion is bad and I put makeup on to cover a mark, Tara always notices. She will ask, "Mama, do you have a boo boo? Can I kiss it?" More embarrassing still is when we go out and she makes sure that everyone else knows that Mama has a boo boo and that they, too, should kiss it. What can I do but laugh and be touched by her concern?

One day, Sumant was preparing for an important meeting, a presentation that he had been working on for weeks. During the break, he was reviewing his notes, while his colleagues checked their phone messages and e-mails. Suddenly, he found that they were looking at him awkwardly. Sumant was unaware that he was humming "Rubber Duckie," Ernie's favorite song from *Sesame Street,* to himself. He laughed when one of the other men started to hum along with him!

What special gifts of laughter and lightheartedness our children give us! They teach us through these moments that nothing is as important as smiling, loving, and enjoying our lives to the fullest.

34

I promise to teach you
the power of forgiveness.

One evening my grandparents were at home having dinner when three young men burst through the door. They were wearing ski masks and had machine guns in their hands. They had knocked my grandparents' servant unconscious and charged into the house where my grandparents were enjoying a quiet evening together.

The men ordered Maa and Daddy to get up, open up the safes in the house, and give over their jewelry, money, and other valuable possessions. My grandparents, who were both in their seventies at the time, had to move slowly, but they followed all instructions, knowing that the only way to save their own lives was not to resist. At this time in Delhi, there had been a number of break-ins, and many of them had ended up in tragedy. So far, the men had only spoken roughly to my grandparents but had not touched or forced them in any other way.

After my grandparents emptied out all of the closets, the ringleader ordered one of the other men to kill them. When he hesitated, Daddy, who had remained calm and totally aware, noticed that the young man was shaking and, he thought, actually crying. The young man then stood up to the ringleader and said he could not do that.

Instead, he would just tie my grandparents up in the bathroom. The young man noted that they were old and helpless, and it would do them no good to kill the elderly couple. He made his case, and the ringleader gruffly told him to quickly put them away, while the others stashed the goods in the car.

The young man then took my grandmother's hand and helped her to the bathroom as my grandfather walked in front of them. As the young man sat my grandparents down on the toilet and the tub, he lightly tied the rope around their hands. Once again, my grandfather observed that the young man was trembling from silent sobs. "Beta," my grandfather asked using the familiar term for son, "why do you engage in such horrific crimes?" The man tenuously replied, "I have no other way to support my family, Doctor Saab. My father is now gone, and I have my mother, wife, and three young children to feed. There are no jobs, and I cannot let them starve."

Sharp as ever, my grandfather picked up on the boy's respectful reference to him as Doctor Saab. "Beta, have we met before?" my grandfather gently asked. Suddenly all the pent-up emotion that the boy had been holding back came flowing out. He began to cry, saying, "If only God can ever forgive me. Doctor Saab, several years ago you performed heart surgery on my father. You saved his life at the time. I only recognized you when we entered the house. You never charged us a penny, and now I have committed the greatest sin against you." And then he took off his mask, and as tears rolled down his face, he bent down and first touched Daddy's feet and then Maa's. "Please, please forgive me." My grandmother touched his head, accepting his gesture of respect, and said, "God be with you, my son." And with that, the man ran out of the house to escape with his comrades.

Later that week, the police captured three young men who had staged an armed robbery in a house in a neighboring colony. My grandparents were called to see if they could identify the young men, and it turned out that they were in fact the same. The boys were locked up to await trial, as the prosecution built up their case against them. They had committed robberies in several areas, one of them ending up in the hospitalization of the victims.

When it came time for the trial, my grandparents were called to testify against the criminals. Maa, however, refused. Her heart had been torn by the struggle of the young man, and she could not stop thinking about his mother, wife, and young children. She knew they would be punished (which they were), and she felt that her incrimination would add nothing new to the case.

Instead, Maa, without telling anyone, tracked down the young man's family. She gave his wife some money to buy some food and books for the children's schooling. She embraced the man's mother and consoled her over her son's actions. Daddy had saved his father's life, and now Maa was saving the lives of those that he had loved.

35

I promise to help you see that happiness is not dependent on circumstances.

One notion that our parents always tried to instill in us was the concept of self-referal. By listening to our hearts and our inner voices, rather than the chorus of opinions, situations, and circumstances that change every moment, we learned to remain centered, confident, secure, and happy. Our parents used the following parable to teach us this lesson.

In ancient China, there was an old man who lived in a small village. The old man had a son who had gone to the city to try to find some work. The other villagers thought that the man must be sad to be alone, but he never expressed any loneliness or sadness about his situation.

One day, the old man's son returned home. The villagers went to congratulate him, but they were surprised to see a lack of emotion at what they thought were good tidings. The old man was neither happy nor sad, and he just thanked them for their interest.

A few days later, the old man was going for a walk with his horse when the reins escaped from his hand and the horse ran away. Upon hearing the news, the villagers went to his house and consoled him on the loss of such a fine horse. The old man thanked them, but he didn't show any sadness.

The next day, the villagers were surprised to see that the horse had returned, and with it were two of the most magnificent black mares they had ever seen. The villagers were even more shocked, however, to see the lack of excitement in the old man when they went to congratulate him. He didn't seem to rejoice in the good luck that had been bestowed on him.

A week later, the old man's son was trying to tame one of the mares, when he fell and broke his leg. When the villagers went to check on the boy, they could not understand why the old man did not weep at his son's fate.

Later that day, the local army came to town to recruit all the able-bodied boys for a battle. When the army reached the old man's house, they decided not to take the boy because of his broken leg. When the villagers went to congratulate the old man, he smiled at them and simply said, "Whatever happens, always happens for the best."

36

I promise to help you see that some of the most important lessons in your life can be learned from your darkest, most challenging moments.

During my first year of business school, Sumant and I developed an idea for a start-up company called MyPotential. It was the heyday of the Internet boom, and our idea—to create a media home for the self-development industry—was quickly adopted by my father, and in turn a barrage of partners, investors, and high-profile managers. The next two years proved to be a total whirlwind of experience, emotions, and dramatic successes and failures.

MyPotential proved to be a turning point in my life. As the designated and public founder of the company, I dropped out of business school, moved to Los Angeles while Sumant stayed in school in Chicago, traveled the country to meet with potential investors, ultimately raised more than ten million dollars, and became the first employee of the company. Over the next eighteen months, MyPotential grew to more than sixty employees and was identified as one of the companies to watch in the coming years. We attracted some of the most respected business people as investors and advisors, and we were featured in media around the world. Those first few months were some of the most exciting in our lives, as Sumant and I were young entrepreneurs who slowly saw our business school vision grow into something truly tremendous.

However, with that success also came an onslaught of new challenges, and soon enough, we realized that we no longer had control over the vision or execution of the company. The reins had been taken over by "wiser, more experienced," professionals. We were pushed to the side as others "who knew better" made the important decisions regarding the direction of the company.

The biggest challenge presented itself when we hired a manager whose vision, style, and approach was in complete contrast to mine. This proved to be one of the most stressful relationships I have ever had in my life. As the designated senior manager of the company, this person came to MyPotential and correctly realized that there were many weaknesses and things that needed to be changed. Her style, however, was direct, nonemotional, and at times so harsh that people would break down in tears during meetings with her. All in all, she was with the company for three months, but in that short period of time, my entire world seemed to crumble.

In retrospect, I can look upon this time as a critical crossroads in my life. I see how my fear of confrontation and insecurities about my abilities paralyzed me from making a stand for what I believed in. I lost my voice and was stifled by fear. I watched as people I had hired and empowered left the company brokenhearted, despondent, and angry. These were people who had joined MyPotential because they believed in our vision, goals, and passion. As a result, I slowly witnessed the unraveling of my dream because I was too scared to speak and state my opinion when I knew something was wrong. It forced me to examine myself in a way I had never done before, to admit to my deepest fears and accept and embrace my strengths and weaknesses.

I can genuinely say that today I am grateful to this woman, who forced me to look deep into myself. In many ways, she helped me discover my voice.

Ultimately, the hurt nurtured a new passion in me—a commitment to make sure that I am heard in the future and that I am not stifled by fear or thinking that someone else knows better or can do something that I cannot do.

And most important, through my own example, I can sow the seeds of confidence in my children so they will voice their opinions and do, with strength and conviction, what they know in their hearts to be right.

Murakumo ya—	*The clustering clouds—*
Tsuki no kuma wo ba	*Can it be they wipe away*
Nogofuramu?	*The lunar shadows?*
Hareyuku tabi ni	*Every time they clear a bit*
Terimasaru kana.	*The moonlight shines the brighter.*

By Minamoto no Toshiyori

Reflection

REMEMBER A CHALLENGE you faced with an adversary. Think about how that experience made you a stronger person. Make a commitment to share this story with your baby one day.

37

I promise to help you avoid preconceived notions about how things are supposed to be.

As individuals, we are constantly making judgments about people, places, and situations. As parents, our judgments leave deeply rooted impressions on our children that form the basis of how they view the world. We help shape their fears, biases, and hopes, and we set the foundations for what they dream. The following African folktale about a baby frog and a baby snake who share a special day of friendship reminds me of our responsibilities as parents and our power to influence the minds of our children.

Baby Frog was practicing his hopping one afternoon by a marsh. "Hop, pop, hop!" he croaked to himself as he jumped from one stone to another. There was such a sense of freedom every time he leapt from the ground.

As he hopped along, Baby Frog saw a long, thin creature twisting by the bush. "Slither, slide, slither!" hissed the creature.

"Who are you?" asked Baby Frog.

"I am Baby Snake," the snake replied.

"Would you like to play with me today?" Baby Frog asked.

"Yes," replied the snake.

And so they hopped and slithered all day long in the bush. Baby Frog showed Baby Snake how to hop from one stone to another. It was a bit hard for Baby Snake given his length, but he had fun nonetheless.

And then Baby Snake showed Baby Frog how to slide up a twig on the bush. Going up was a bit difficult, but Baby Frog found that it tickled to slide on his round belly.

They giggled together as they played.

Soon enough, Baby Frog and Baby Snake got hungry and decided to go home for lunch. They promised to meet again tomorrow so that they could play.

As Baby Frog headed home, his mother saw him in the most awkward position. "What are you doing?" she asked.

"Look, Mama!" Baby Frog boasted as he hopped, slithered, hopped, and slid along. "My friend, Baby Snake, taught me how to slide this morning!" he said proudly.

Mama Frog's eyes bulged out with fear. "Baby, don't you know that the snakes eat us? Promise me you will never play with him again!"

When Baby Snake arrived home, his mother laughed at first. "What on earth are you doing?" she asked, as Baby snake contorted from side to side and up and down.

"Hopping, Mama, look!" Baby Snake proudly replied. Slither, slide, hop, and pop. "My friend Baby Frog taught me how!" he smiled.

Mama snake hissed. "Baby, the frogs are our food, not our friends. Next time you see him, you swallow him up. And don't hop like that—you look silly!"

The next morning, when Baby Frog and Baby Snake went to the marsh, they kept their distance. Baby Frog hopped back a bit and told Baby Snake that he could not play with him anymore. "Thanks for teaching me how to slide. I really enjoyed it," he said sadly.

Baby Snake thought about what his mama had told him about eating the frog, but he remembered how much fun he had yesterday and slithered away.

As he slid away, Baby Snake sadly looked back. "Thanks for teaching me how to hop!" he said.

In secret, at different ends of the marsh, both Baby Frog and Baby Snake would practice—slide, hop, slither, and pop—and remember the one day of friendship that had been so much fun for both of them.

38

I promise to teach you
not to take life too seriously.

My father's life motto, which he passed on to Gotham and me, is, "Never take life too seriously." While the words may sound simple and lighthearted, even cliché, following this guidance is often much harder than one would think.

For me, the lesson has taken on its own flavor. Not taking life too seriously has meant not getting offended by anyone else, not holding grudges, and forgiving others. It has meant being able to laugh at myself and admitting that I am wrong at times. It has also meant controlling my anger because at times it is so easy and fulfilling to lash out at others.

Often, getting offended is largely a reaction to thinking that one is too important and imagining that someone must give me respect because of who I am, not what I have done or how I act. I have seen others get offended because someone did not talk to them in the right way, observe a custom, or follow a rule. When I get offended, it is because there is a part of me that actually agrees with the criticism or feels that somehow the perceived look or slight was justified in some way.

I also have seen that it is easy to hold grudges. By holding a grudge, we can often avoid conflict, and we can blame someone else for things that have gone wrong. We can avoid facing our own demons and insecurities, because that is a very difficult thing to do. It is much easier to take our anger out on others.

Another important lesson is that we cannot take ourselves too seriously. It is okay to get upset and angry, to feel insecure and inept, and to need approval and seek solace. We should let ourselves experience the disappointments, anger, and frustration, and we should share our feelings with those close to us. And once we go through that process, it is important to let go, to move on, and to laugh again. There are too many beautiful, funny, and special things in this world to let seriousness get the best of us.

There is a story in my family about my grandmother's sister who did not talk to her family for more than forty years because she interpreted a statement made by her father as an insult. (He had told her that because her daughters were not so attractive, she should educate them well, so they could care for themselves rather than waiting to find husbands.) There are so many ways to interpret that statement, yet because my grandmother's sister took offense, she and her children missed out on a lifelong relationship with her family. When her father died and she finally reached out to her siblings, we discovered a whole new set of cousins who we are now close to. As two generations removed from the original incident, we can laugh about it and be grateful that we have each other.

39

I promise to empower you to trust yourself.

As parents, our words have drastic consequences on our children's perceptions of their strengths and weaknesses. We are generally aware of how our comments shape their worldviews, but one thing we cannot control are the comments that they hear from others. Thus, we need to teach them the power of trusting themselves and the ability to prevent others from swaying them from their beliefs and values. This classic Aesop fable illustrates this concept beautifully.

Once upon a time, a fox was sleuthing around the forest when he came across three crows, each with a piece of cheese in its mouth. The fox was hungry, but he realized that he needed to be a bit smart about getting the cheese from the crows because he could not climb up to the high branches on which they sat.

The first crow was about to eat her cheese when the fox called up to her, saying "Beautiful, beautiful crow. I have never seen a bird so lovely in all my life." The crow, hearing such compliments from below, looked down and suddenly became very conscious of her posture and hoped her feathers looked combed. She saw the fox, who was gazing admiringly up at her. She flew down to a lower branch to hear the fox better. "Oh, now I can see you even better," the fox said. "How fine your feathers are! And never have I seen such a perfect beak. I can only imagine what a heavenly voice you have." Eager to please her admirer, the crow opened her mouth to sing, and out dropped the cheese. Quickly, the fox scooped it up and swallowed the delicious treat. The first crow realized that she had been tricked, but it was too late because the cheese was gone.

The second crow watched this interaction and fumed in anger. How dare the fox trick his friend like that! The fox turned to the second crow, realizing the bird was glaring at him. "What are you looking at, you ugly crow?" the fox asked. "Boy, I have never seen anything so dirty as you are! Are your feathers actually that dark or is it that they are so filled with dirt they look that ugly? How do you have any friends? They must have to hold their noses every time they go near you!" As the fox ranted on, the second crow got angrier and angrier. He had always been a bit sensitive about his dark feathers, but how dare the fox insinuate that he was dirty? He was very meticulous about his cleanliness. Intent to set the fox straight, the second crow opened his beak to shout back. But before a sound came, out fell the piece of cheese. In an instant, the fox swallowed it up.

Now the fox approached the third crow. The third crow had watched the interchange between his comrades and the fox with little emotion or interest. He was just sad that they had missed out on such a lovely treat. The fox now began an aggressive pitch, trying to get the third crow to respond in anger.

"You think you are better than your friends, do you?" the fox asked. "What does a stupid crow like you know about anything in life? You sit there watching the world like you don't care. I think it's because you know you are too weak to do anything."

The crow smiled down at the fox and slowly began chewing his piece of cheese. The fox now changed tactics, almost desperate in his plea. "Maybe I misjudged you. You are a smart one after all. I bet if we partnered together, we could rule this forest. What do you think, my friend?" But the third crow was unaffected and continued to chew his wonderful treat.

The fox and the other crows watched the third crow with envy as he finished the cheese.

40

I promise to help you always reach for the stars.

When my parents found out that my mother was pregnant with me, they were thrilled but also under a lot of pressure. My father was doing his post-medical training, and they had very little money in their pockets. They had arrived in the United States several months earlier with $8. My mother was twenty-one, and my father was twenty-three. They calculated that it would cost about $800 to deliver a baby in the United States. This was an astronomical amount of money for them.

My parents sat with their friends to discuss how they could afford to deliver the baby. Everyone offered to pitch in to help with the expenses, yet it would still be a stretch. Finally, one of my uncles came up with a brilliant idea. It would cost less to buy a ticket to India ($200 at the time) than to deliver the baby in the United States. If they combined their money, they could comfortably buy a one-way ticket to India and then my grandparents could send my mother back from there. Relieved, my dad popped a bottle of champagne, and they celebrated the prospect of a new baby.

In the midst of the celebration, however, another uncle suddenly hushed everyone. "This won't work," he said. "If the baby is born in India, it will not be able to run for president of the United States." There was complete silence, and a sense of confusion filled the room. My parents' faces fell as the repercussions of this statement hit them. Their child, if born outside the United States, could never run for president. This was very serious. As new immigrants, America was the land of opportunity. How could they take such an opportunity away from their beloved child?

For the next few days, my parents and their friends struggled with the decision about where to deliver the baby. One morning my father received a call from my uncle, who said he had thought about it long and hard. He pointed out to my father that Henry Kissinger could never run for president either, yet look at the influence he had on world affairs. Henry Kissinger was admired around the world.

This argument made sense, and my parents were quite relieved. Realistically, they could not afford to have the baby in the United States. They collected all their money, borrowed some from their friends, and my mother boarded a plane for India.

While my parents had been forced to make a small sacrifice for their child, they maintained a vision for the great things she could achieve. It was this vision that nurtured the confidence in me that I have the potential to achieve anything.

Reflection

SPEND A FEW MOMENTS thinking about how you can empower your child so that your child knows that he or she can achieve anything. Think of role models and leaders who have changed the world and make a commitment to tell your child their inspiring stories.

Values

How to treat yourself and others

41

I promise to show you how values can be the basis for genuine success.

An important lesson that our parents taught us when we were young was to develop a sense of values that could drive everything else we did in our lives. These values were not dictated or told to us, but rather, like all children, we watched how our parents treated others and themselves.

As we grew older, my father encouraged Gotham and me to begin a process of actually defining our values. This exercise made our value system a conscious part of our everyday thinking and activities. As we grew up, our values drove our academic, professional, and personal decisions and relationships.

Every morning as part of our meditation, we would think about the most valuable experiences that we wanted to have during the day. These experiences could include friendship, love, peace, harmony, laughter, creativity, intuition, discovery, and more. When we were silent and truly listened to our hearts, we always found that our most valued experiences were ones that made us feel good, happy, secure, and loved.

We would then take a few seconds to contemplate how we could find and nurture these experiences. Inevitably, the process of discovering our experiences would entail giving, sharing, or creating those experiences with others. This created a dynamic where we always felt connected to others and motivated to treat others in the same way that we would want to be treated. It also created a vision that engaged others who wanted success and fulfillment as much as we did. And most important, it allowed us to shape our own destinies, focusing on the experiences that would keep us inspired, creative, and passionate about each new day.

As parents, we hope we can instill values in our children that will give them confidence and inspire them to treat others with love and respect. The simple exercise described above is a powerful way to help children listen to what makes them feel good and then seek out and share those feelings with others in their world.

Reflection

NAME TEN VALUES that you hold most dear. Promise your child that you will teach these values to him or her by your own example.

42

I promise to show you that your adversary is not so different from yourself.

On August 14, 1997, the eve of fifty years of independence for India from the British Empire, I made a pilgrimage to the border of Pakistan. Setting out before dusk, I boarded a crowded train in New Delhi for Amritsar, a city near the border. We were a party of four—Radhika, my young cousin; Rahul Bose, an Indian actor; Rajeev Sethi, an acclaimed activist and artist; and myself. As we got on the train, we were each silent, lost in our own thoughts about what this journey meant to us.

August 15, 1947, was one of the greatest moments in the twentieth century. The Indian sub-continent had been subjugated by the British for more than 200 years until India overcame its oppressor through the iron will of the masses. Through peaceful protests and a determination not to accept the oppression of the British, the people of South Asia beat a powerful ruler under the leadership of Mahatma Gandhi. It was a time of celebration, victory, honor, and strength.

But for many, including my family, it was a time of violence, displacement, and great sorrow. My grandparents and their brothers and sisters were living in Sialkot, a town in Punjab, which had been designated a part of Pakistan by a random line drawn on a map by the British and other peace negotiators. Sialkot and the neighboring villages, which were mostly Muslim, would now become another country, and my family, who were Hindus, would be forced to leave their home and move to a new land. In a night of riots, mayhem, and passionate mobs, my grandmother's brother, a respected policeman, was shot in the head by a Muslim mob that wanted vengeance for another death. The rest of the family, panicked and scared for their lives, joined millions of other refugees and headed west to find protection and peace in independent India. During those weeks of liberation, more than 1 million people died.

As our train departed the hustle and bustle of Delhi, I tried to imagine the mix of joy, freedom, sorrow, and loss that my grandparents and their peers must have felt fifty years ago. I tried to think about what it must have been like for them to participate in the jubilant celebrations as the British departed, while also mourning the loss of their family, friends, homes, and roots. The reality was that many of their closest friends were Muslims. They had lived side by side for generations, and together they shared more similarities than differences.

I thought about how that rift had carried on generations later. Two of Sumant's closest friends, Jaffer and Shazad, are Pakistanis. The three of them went to the same college in the United States, spending their most formative years together. They spoke the same language, shared many of the same customs, and ate the same food. While Jaffer and Shazad both come from Muslim families, their philosophy of life, their approach to family and friends, and their values are the same as ours. The first person Sumant called when we got engaged was Jaffer. Yet when Jaffer applied for a visa to attend our wedding, he was turned away because India and Pakistan are enemies.

That night in 1997, more than 50,000 Indians sang, danced, and celebrated, waiting for our neighbors on the other side of the border to join us. Every person held a candle representing our hopes for peace and friendship. However, no one showed up on the other side, and we could not hide our disappointment.

The next day, we heard on the news that thousands of Pakistanis had attempted to join us there to be part of the celebration. They had been held up on the other side by border control because of fear that things could turn violent. Nonetheless, they had come.

Our journey to the border provided the first step, as individual citizens, toward creating a bridge with a people who we had been told were our enemies. While we had faced disappointment that our moment was not as dramatic as we had hoped, we found some solace in the fact that the outreach had been reciprocated.

I realized that it is important to take a first step independent of immediate results. It is that first step that sets in motion more deeply rooted and lasting change.

43

I promise to teach you
about selfless compassion.

Once upon a time in a small village, there lived a dancing girl named Vasava-datta. She was the most beautiful and talented dancer that people had seen in generations, and they traveled from the far ends of the country to see her dance. Vasavadatta's divine and graceful movements seduced men, women, and children and made them forget about all their troubles and feel happy and secure. Vasavadatta was given jewels and rich saris by her many suitors, who would compete for her attention by writing poetry for her and singing her praises. Despite all this, Vasavadatta refused to marry until her heart was swept away by love.

One day, Vasavadatta was walking down the street when she saw a young monk sleeping. As Vasavadatta approached the monk, she saw that he was the most gentle and beautiful man she had ever seen. Instantaneously, she fell in love with him. This was the feeling she had been waiting for. Breathless and dizzy with love, Vasavadatta began to dance the most beautiful and seductive dance she had ever danced.

Hearing the jingling of the bells on her feet, the young monk, Upagupta, awoke to see the beautiful Vasavadatta swirling before him. As he stirred, Vasavadatta smiled at him and said, "Young man, there is no need for you to sleep on the streets.

Come to my house and be my guest tonight. I will take care of all your needs." The monk returned a gracious and gentle smile and said, "Not now, but when the time is right, I promise that I will come."

Several years later, the monk was walking in the same village when he stumbled upon a homeless woman sleeping on a street corner. Her clothes were torn, her eyes were bloodshot, and she had wounds all over her body. She coughed, breathed heavily, and shivered in pain.

The monk gently picked her up in his arms and took her to the monastery. There he cleaned her wounds, stroked and fed her, and gave her a blanket to warm her shivering body. Touched by the compassion of this stranger, Vasavadatta looked up at the monk and asked, "Who are you, merciful one, that takes care of me with so much tenderness and compassion?" And Upagupta replied, "I promised you long ago that when the time was right, I would come. Rest and heal now. I am here."

44

I promise to show you the beauty
that comes from loving others.

One summer day, when Gotham and I were playing in our backyard, we found two kittens. They were spotted black and white, with the most precious faces, soft purrs, and gentle natures. They were so tiny that I could hold both in the cup of my small ten-year-old hands. Upon closer inspection, we saw that the kittens were both scratched and bleeding, and it seemed that they were very frightened.

We begged our mother to allow us to bring the kittens into the house. She was a bit hesitant because she could not assess if they belonged to someone else, had any sort of disease, and were safe to bring inside. In the end, our mother agreed to let us set up a little basket outside on the porch for the kittens. That way, if the mother cat or owner was looking for them, they would easily find them. We put a cushion in the basket, and we set the little kittens inside. We cleaned their wounds and put out a small bowl of warm milk. The kittens lapped it up in a minute, and they were soon sound asleep. As Gotham and I gazed at the kittens, we decided to name them Luv and Kush after two young brothers whom we adored from Indian mythology.

For the next week, we became totally obsessed with Luv and Kush. I would wake up at night, nervous that they were not okay, and sneak downstairs to look out the window to check on them. One evening, I heard on the news that it was going to rain that night so I cried to my mother that we had no choice but to bring the kittens into the house. She agreed to put them in the garage. Day by day, Luv and Kush grew stronger, more playful, and more mischievous. They loved to tangle themselves up in yarn, paw at a tennis ball, and skip around following our waving hands. When the kittens slept, they cuddled close together in deep breathing slumber, secure next to each other's warm bodies.

It became apparent to my parents after about a week that Luv and Kush were truly lost or abandoned. After talking with an animal shelter, my mother approached us with the news that we would have to give the kittens to the shelter to make sure that they did not carry any infections. We pleaded with her to let us keep them for just a while longer, but she held her ground, explaining that the kittens did not belong to us and needed professional care. We were devastated, and the night before taking them to the nursery was a sleepless one for me.

The next day, we picked up Luv and Kush's carefully tailored basket, and we took them to the shelter. With tears in my eyes, I told the shelter worker how they liked their milk and where they slept on the pillow. I kept the yarn in the basket, as well as a new soft ball on which I had written, "We Love You." As we drove away, I cried and cried, feeling that a part of my soul was being torn away from me.

Gotham and I were so depressed and angry at our parents, not able to understand the risks that were involved in hosting abandoned kittens in our house. I thought I would never be able to forgive them, until a call came two days later from the animal shelter. They told my mother that they had found Luv and Kush's owners, who were so grateful for all we had done for the baby kittens. I was crushed. I had been hoping that we could formally adopt the kittens, and I closed myself in my room and cried in my bed.

Later that evening, my parents knocked on my door. They called Gotham, who at seven was emulating my mood, and presented a proposal to us. They had seen how much we had cared for Luv and Kush, and they were impressed with our responsible and caring attitude. We could not have Luv and Kush anymore, so they asked how did we feel about getting a puppy? I could not believe my ears, and my wet eyes now shed a new sort of tear. These were tears of happiness and absolute love for my parents—already I could imagine the little fur ball who would become our puppy, Nicholas.

I went to bed thanking Luv and Kush for giving Gotham and I such a lovely gift. They had opened up our hearts, and because of them, we would now be getting the puppy I had been dreaming about.

45

I promise to remember the importance of humility.

"Move!"

Hanuman, the monkey god, turned to see who it was that spoke to him so rudely.

A big man with wide shoulders stood in front of him, his hands on his hips. "Well!" he said. Hanuman laughed. It was Bhima, the strongest man on earth. He used his strength to help those in need, and he had recently rid a cursed village of an evil demon. The demon had been frightening people for years, and no one had been able to defeat him—except Bhima. Hanuman laughed again and turned his back to Bhima.

"Don't laugh at me, you stupid monkey. Just get out of my way," Bhima said. He couldn't believe the monkey's nerve. Most people would not only move out of his way when they saw him coming, but they would also bow to him. Meanwhile, Hanuman could not believe Bhima's stupidity. *He has no idea who I am*, Hanuman thought.

And he was right. Bhima didn't realize the monkey was the great Hanuman, one of the most respected gods on earth and in the heavens. He was also known to be one of the kindest.

It's nice that people like me, Hanuman thought. *But why don't people like each other?*

Hanuman had seen people be rude to one another long enough. Bhima was the last straw. *Well,* thought Hanuman, *It's time to teach him a lesson.*

"Did you hear me or are you deaf? I said move!" yelled Bhima. After Bhima had demanded that the monkey move for the fourth time. Hanuman turned and said, "But can't you see, I am weak. My bones ache when I try to move. I can see though that you are strong. Why don't you move me?" Bhima rolled his eyes and said, "Just move out of the way, you lazy, no good monkey."

Infuriated, Bhima bent down to throw the monkey and his tail aside. To his surprise, the tail would not budge. As hard as Bhima pushed, pulled, shoved, and kicked, he could not get the monkey to move. Within minutes, Bhima broke out in a sweat, and try as hard as he could, he could not move the monkey even one inch. At last he had to give up. Deflated and defeated, Bhima realized how obnoxious he had been and that he had underestimated the power of the monkey.

The monkey smiled, casually got up, and cleared the entrance. In that instant, Bhima saw Hanuman in his true divine form, as the great and strong monkey god. He understood that Hanuman had been teaching him a lesson. Humbled, Bhima bowed before the monkey god and apologized before entering the cave. He made a promise never to treat another being without the respect that he would offer a god.

Reflection

WHAT ARE THE MOST IMPORTANT qualities that you hope for in your child? Why are these important to you?

46

I promise to teach you about the sanctity of friendship.

Bhara Papa, Sumant's grandfather, was best friends with his landlord. The two men had gotten married around the same time, their wives were like sisters, and their children grew up together. Every afternoon, the two friends had a tradition of sitting together for tea to gossip about the day, their families, and the state of the world. Sumant's mother and her siblings would address the landlord in the same way they would their father's real brother.

The laws of governing property in India were going through many changes in those days, and a discrepancy developed over how much rent Sumant's grandfather owed his friend. His friend actually let it pass for years because his relationship with Bhara Papa was more important to him than the extra bit of cash. But, one day, the landlord was confronted by his sons, who felt that their father was being cheated out of a sizable amount of income. Without telling their father, they had issued a lawsuit in the courts against Bhara Papa to demand higher rent. The landlord himself was devastated by this news, but he was unwilling to turn his back on his sons.

So began years and years of a court case to determine the right amount of rent. And so ended years of a precious friendship that had served as a foundation in the two men's lives. With the awkwardness of the lawsuit and the way in which it was issued, Bhara Papa was angry, and the landlord did not want to put his sons in a bad light. The two men no longer sat for their afternoon tea, and they began to lead separate lives, avoiding each other at the entrance of the building. They banned their wives from seeing each other.

Most tragically, when Sumant's mother got married, the landlord and his family were not invited to the wedding. This was truly sad because the landlord's wife had watched Sumant's mother grow up almost as one of her own children. The landlord's wife hid behind a beam with tears rolling down her face as she watched Sumant's mother leave for her wedding. She quietly asked a servant to run and anonymously give a packet to Sumant's grandmother containing a gift for Sumant's mother. When Sumant's mother opened the packet, she found one of her dear friend's most valued and treasured pieces of jewelry.

For years, the two men continued to go to court each week, struggling through the bureaucracy of the system to get the case settled. They awkwardly looked at each other, each one wanting to ask how the other one was, but holding back because of appearance and ego.

Finally, one afternoon as Bhara Papa was sitting in his car to drive to the courthouse, his landlord knocked on the car window. As Bhara Papa rolled down the window, his landlord put his hands together as a sign of respect and said, "I was wondering if you would give me a ride to the courthouse. It seems such a waste of petrol for both of us to drive to the same place." Bhara Papa nodded his head and told him to get in the car. They drove to the courthouse in silence, but the first barrier had been broken down.

And so began a new tradition of driving together to the courthouse every week to fight each other in court. Slowly, the two men began to talk, catch up on recent events, and share stories about their children and other goings on in their days.

Before long, each man would look forward to the weekly court hearings, leaving just a little bit earlier every time so that they could have some extra time to talk.

47

I promise to play with you forever.

As Gotham and I grew older and more mature, our parents were undergoing their own transformation. In many ways, they were becoming less serious, more carefree, and more secure about their place in the world.

The high stress of being new immigrants in a new country, my father's sleepless nights as a young resident, the loneliness my mother faced raising two kids virtually alone while my dad worked all the time, and our financial struggles all began to ease as the years passed. The hard work, perseverance, and growing community of friends and family in the United States gave our parents a sense of security that allowed them to blossom more as individuals. Their spiritual journey that began with meditation and evolved into my father's career as an author, speaker, and world leader also provided a happier, new phase for them.

In many ways, Gotham and I really became friends with our father during these later years when he was less stressed and happier and more relaxed with his place in the world. In fact, we found that our dad was often the playful one, making us laugh or try something new. When we were with him, we were usually engaged in some new sort of game or adventure.

Some of my favorite memories from my teenage years are from skiing trips with my family. Gotham, my father, and I would take skiing lessons together and then race each other down the mountain. We would then meet my mother for lunch, each of us boasting to her about who was the best among us. Of course, my father was always most eager to impress her, and his tall tales would make us all laugh until we were breathless.

One afternoon, we waited in line for the ski lift. As is the custom, people called out, "Single? Single?" looking for a partner to ride with up to the top of the mountain. My father responded seriously by saying, "No. Very happily married for over fifteen years. Here are my kids!" At this stage, Gotham and I had got used to laughing at our father rather than being embarrassed by him, and we enjoyed watching the confused skiers try to figure out how to respond to him.

When we reached the top of the mountain, we challenged each other to a race. We each headed down, and I soon lost Gotham and Papa, focusing solely on the slopes ahead. When I reached the bottom, Gotham had beaten me to the finish line, but my father was not to be found. So we waited, planning how we would tease him. We waited and waited and waited.

After about half an hour, my father reached the bottom of the slope. He was completely covered in snow, white flakes covering his hat, gloves, goggles, jacket, and every part of his body. Gotham and I immediately asked if he had fallen, and he immediately responded, "No! Never!" He proceeded to tell us about a man who had totally wiped out on the slope and potentially broken a leg. Our father had been compelled to stop and help the man until the emergency patrol came over. He said we should really be treating him as a hero rather than teasing him, and he challenged us to another race. Gotham and I looked at each other speculatively, but our father maintained his straight face, and we began to believe him.

As we waited in line to go up the ski lift again, a young guy approached our father. "Dude," he said, "That was a massive fall you had up there. It's amazing you didn't break a leg. Are you okay?" Our father meekly replied that he was fine. He then turned to Gotham and, with mischief in his eyes, said, "He must have mistaken me for the other man. You know, he had a similar jacket."

Gotham and I burst out laughing, but our father kept to his story. When we began our next race, his determined expression made Gotham and me laugh so much that we could not focus on the race, and Papa beat us to the finish line.

48

I promise to show you
the power of pure intention.

In India, the new year, Diwali, is marked by lights, games, and festivities around the country. Diwali is a time when we honor the goddess Lakshmi, who provides good luck and fortune to those who worship her.

On Diwali, we light candles and lamps in and around our houses as signals to Lakshmi that we are thinking about her on this night. The legend goes that she will visit your house and bless you and your family.

There is a story about a very wealthy man who wanted to create the biggest spectacle that the world had ever seen on Diwali. It was a way in which he could demonstrate his wealth, gloat about all his success, and show others that they could never compete with him when it came to attracting Lakshmi's affection. The man had special lights made from every corner of the earth, and he even created a fireworks show that lit up the skies above. The entire village came to see his show, and undoubtedly there were many in the crowd who were jealous about his fortune. In their minds, there was no question that Lakshmi must love this man who could create such a celebration for her.

The man had a servant woman who lived across the alley behind his house. The woman had one son, but he was ill, and she struggled daily to provide him with food and nutrition. Her master treated her and his other staff badly; he paid them miniscule wages because he knew that they were desperate for anything that they could get. Even though he was one of the wealthiest men in the world, he would not give her any extra money for medication for her ailing son.

The woman also wanted to show her dedication to Lakshmi that night, but she could not afford to buy anything to make light. She saw the lights of the man's palatial house shimmering in the night and the fireworks flash in the sky. Nonetheless, she was not distracted from her mission. While making her son's dinner, she realized that she had only enough oil to make a portion of food for herself or to make a candle. Without hesitation, she made some dinner for her son and set aside the remaining oil. She found some wax and made the simplest of candles.

That night as the man presented the grandest spectacle the world had ever seen, the woman set the small candle in her window. She quietly said her prayers and went to sleep.

The next morning, the wealthy man jumped out of bed to discover piles of newspapers reporting on his party. He also woke up to a pile of bills that had to be paid. On the other side of the alley, however, the woman woke up to find a true gift from the gods. Her son jumped out of bed, looking vibrant and healthy. Miraculously, he was better. That day, as her son was out in the market, he was approached by a businessman looking for an apprentice. The businessman offered the young man a job. Now the woman and her son would no longer suffer. Lakshmi had blessed their family for their humbleness, dedication, and purity.

49

I promise to teach you that human dignity is a fundamental right.

After Sumant and I got married, we lived in India for several years. While I had visited India almost every year growing up, living there was a completely new experience for me, and it was quite challenging at times.

While India is one of the most colorful, spiritual, dynamic, and vibrant places on earth, cities like New Delhi are also very polluted, corrupt, overpopulated and frustrating. Time in India seems to run at a slower pace, space is conceived differently, and the urgency that we often feel in the Western world is muted in a way that can be unbearable for a foreigner.

After one particularly frustrating day, Sumant and I were having dinner with Prem Uncle (my grandmother's brother) and his wife, Sonia Aunty. We often refer to Prem Uncle as the "Don" of our family because as one of the oldest members of my grandmother's family, he is also one of the wisest. He is one of the more successful businessmen of his generation, and he and Sonia Aunty have always represented all that is classy, smart, and sophisticated to members of our family.

At this dinner, Sumant and I were complaining about India—about the unbearable traffic, the stench of the garbage that was piling up outside our house, the frustration in securing simple documents, and the fear of crime that had recently spiked in our neighborhood. I was so frustrated that I found myself asking Prem Uncle if India was any better now than it had been in the days of the British; perhaps the country would be better suited *not* being a democracy. As soon as I uttered those words, I knew that I had hit a nerve with Prem Uncle. He sat there in silence for a long, unbearable minute before he spoke.

Finally, he slowly and deliberately said, "I am very proud to be Indian, and we as a country have achieved much to be proud about. You children take freedom for granted. As a country, we now know freedom. We shape our own destiny, and we can take responsibility for our successes and our failures. There was a time when those basic rights were taken away from us—when a white man could spit at us if he felt like it, when we had to seek permission to enter our holy places. I proudly witness the frustrations you talk about and know that now we have the power to work on them."

Prem Uncle talked more about the daily oppression his generation and those before him experienced under British rule and how that scarred people to their very souls.

He then reminded us how Mahatma Gandhi empowered people by feeding their hearts, by giving them respect and confidence, by reminding them that they were beneath no one else, and by giving them a dream about what they could achieve. India had set an example for the rest of the world by showing that peaceful protest was a way to effect deeply rooted change. As part of a generation that did not face human rights oppressions, it is easy to forget the battles that those before us fought to ensure our freedom. Prem Uncle had reminded me that my desire to make the world a better place for my children was, in fact, the next chapter in an epic that has been playing for generations.

50

I promise to remember that your passions are just as important as mine.

Boston in the '80s was a grand time if you were a Celtics fan. It was a decade in which the Boston Celtics and the Los Angeles Lakers dominated American basketball, and in which Magic Johnson versus Larry Bird became a defining rivalry.

In many ways, the Celtics/Lakers rivalry provided a forum for our family to connect, celebrate, and bond. Despite my father, mother, and myself not being really interested in sports, my brother's passion for basketball was so extreme that our home seemed to have a Celtics aura about it. Luckily for Gotham, he found a receptive audience for his enthusiasm amongst our cousins and uncles. Gotham would spend hours discussing statistics, trades, speculation, and reviews about past, present, and future games with our other family members. Our house also became the destination for our friends and family to watch games.

My memories of growing up in Boston are very much linked to watching Celtics games on television surrounded by my family. The games became a time I looked forward to because I could expect good food, lots of laughs, and fun afternoons with my cousins, friends, aunts, and uncles. My mother, being the sensitive and perceptive mother that she is, realized early on that sports was one of Gotham's true passions.

Thus, she made every effort to understand the various games, know the players, and support his need to connect with others about the minute details.

For my father, however, Gotham's obsession with sports was somewhat unfathomable. I remember a particular day when we went to Legal Seafood, a popular Boston restaurant, and the entire Philadelphia 76ers team was seated at tables next to us. Gotham was so overwhelmed that he could not speak as he watched many of his heroes eat clam chowder and fish. My father was sincerely upset that Gotham worshipped a young kid who could throw a ball in a hole more than a writer, a doctor, or a social or political activist who was changing the lives of people around the world. Sports did not represent anything in my father's life; his passions were books, medicine, and spirituality. My father just could not understand why Gotham was so obsessed with these players.

In 1987, Bird and Magic faced off in the NBA Finals. The series provided all the drama and excitement that Boston fans could hope for, but ultimately Boston lost to the Lakers in Game Seven when Magic scored a hook shot in the last seconds of the game. Gotham and my cousins were devastated, and a wave of silence and gloom immediately overshadowed the familial gathering at our house. Gotham silently watched the Lakers pop champagne, laughing and dancing at their miraculous victory.

My father, who had been reading a book in another room, walked in to the gloomy atmosphere, realizing that something dramatic had happened. When my uncle told him, my father replied instantly, "But that is impossible. Last night, I put out the intention and visualized Magic Johnson throwing a three pointer in the last few seconds of the game. There is no way the Celtics could lose." We all looked at him in shock, not knowing whether we should react to his visualization coming somewhat true or to the fact that he thought Magic Johnson was on the Celtics.

Gotham immediately broke down in tears and stormed out of the house.

It took many weeks for Gotham to even talk to Papa without remembering the hurt that he had inflicted on him, the city of Boston, and Celtic fans around the world. However, when my father arrived one evening from the hospital with a basketball signed by Larry Bird, Gotham soon began to waver. The next year, Gotham and Papa attended a Celtics game together. Papa was still really not interested in the game, but he did genuinely feign interest for a little while, at least. He realized that it is more important to develop a connection with your child than to judge him.

Reflection

MAKE A COMMITMENT to find ways of connecting with your child. Promise to remain open to new ways of bonding, and let him or her lead in showing ways in which you can connect.

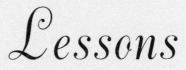

Lessons

Life learning I want to share with you

51

I promise to teach you the power of listening.

As parents, we become very good at telling our children what to do and what not to do. We also strive to teach them to express themselves. Just as important though is for us to show them the power of listening. The following folktale from India is an entertaining way to learn about this important lesson.

It was the birthday of the sun god, and an old woman fasted, prayed, and bathed herself in the sacred waters. It was a splendid day, and she headed to the streets where there were crowds of people cheering at the annual parade of the golden sun chariot. To finish her observances, the old woman had to tell the story of the sun to someone and offer them the blessed rice that she had obtained from the temple.

The old woman first went to her sons because it was her deepest desire that they be blessed during this auspicious day. But her sons were late for a meeting at the court where they had to argue a case about some property, and they rushed away before the old woman could even request their audience. She then approached her granddaughter and her granddaughter's friend, but the girls were busy playing with their dolls and did not want to hear the story. When the old woman found her daughter-in-law, the woman was busy bathing her baby and then had to feed him, so she told the old woman that she could not attend to her now. She then ran into some of her friends, a group of women who were gossiping on their way home from the river where they had been washing clothes. They were not interested in the story, but instead they wanted to hear about who had been at the parade and what they wore. In frustration, the old woman then went to a young boy who was training to be a priest. But the boy was so caught up in his books that he did not want to hear her story. Whoever she turned to would not listen to her story. But the old woman continued her mission to find an audience because her love and devotion to the sun was great.

Finally, the old woman found a poor, pregnant woman who was trying to sell some flowers but was having no luck. With nothing else to do, the flower woman agreed to listen to the story, but just as the old woman began her story, the flower woman fell fast asleep. The old woman, knowing that the day was coming to an end, decided to wait until the flower woman woke up, so she sat on a bench to pass the time.

While waiting, the old woman suddenly heard a voice coming from the womb of the flower woman. Surprised, she listened as the child inside the womb said, "Old woman, I would love to hear your story. Perhaps, you could put the sacred rice on my mother's stomach and tell me about the glorious sun?" So the old woman did just that. She blessed the child, telling her that fortune and happiness would always follow her.

When the old woman returned home, she was surprised to see that all those who had rejected her during the day had seen misfortune. Her sons had lost their court case, her granddaughter's doll had broken, her daughter-in-law had fallen ill, her friends all had fights with their husbands, and the young priest had been scolded by his teachers.

Several months later, the old woman was at home when the flower woman approached with her newborn baby girl. The child was unusually beautiful and had a smile that illuminated the world around her. Her mother told tales of how her business had flourished since the birth of her daughter and that they were moving closer to the palace to open up their own flower stand because of the new-found success. It was there years later that the little girl, now a beautiful young woman, was standing when a handsome prince came by and fell instantly in love with her. As his partner, she became the most adored queen in the kingdom, bearing numerous children, and spreading wealth, good luck, and fortune to all the people in the land.

Reflection

START A DIARY of your favorite fables and folktales that you can share with your child.

52

I promise to teach you that you are never too old to live with passion.

When I first met Dadaji, Sumant's grandfather, I was surprised at how small he was. I had heard such grand stories about him from Sumant, and having met Dadaji's jubilant, energetic, and accomplished children—four boys and two girls—I imagined him to be taller. After all, my husband and his brother, father, and uncles were all six feet tall or taller. Dadaji seemed to be my height. Of course, he was already more than eighty years old by then, and it is said that we shrink with age.

Sumant had told me many stories about his grandfather. He had been born in the 1920s into a very wealthy family. His father, Sumant's great-grandfather, was one of the most successful men in Northwest India. He owned a woolen mill and was recognized as an Indian entrepreneur in colonized India. Later, my father-in-law told me about the letters Sumant's great-grandfather received from Mahatma Gandhi, Rabindranth Tagore, and Pundit Nehru, recognizing him for his achievements. At the age of fifteen, Dadaji had a car, which in the 1930s in India was undoubtedly a rare occurrence. But Dadaji was mostly lost in his books, philosophy, and studying. If he was interested in something, he put his whole heart into it. Dadaji grasped concepts quickly, and if he liked something, he was the best at it. If he wasn't interested in a subject or activity, then he didn't pay attention or pursue it. In this way, Sumant was exactly like him.

Although I heard stories about Dajaji from all his admirers, it wasn't until three years after my marriage that I got to know him for myself. Sumant and I were in Bombay, and Dadaji left work early to spend the afternoon with us. At eighty-three, he still went to his office every day despite being forced to give up driving a year earlier. He refused to miss a day because he refused to get old.

We ordered some tea, and Dadaji asked Sumant and I what we thought about business school and what our plans were for the future. He loved the idea that we were both going to graduate school together and told us to enjoy every moment of it. He asked intelligent questions about what we were learning, wanting us to give him more and more details. Then Dadaji reminded us how the world had changed during his lifetime. When he was a boy, there were no telephones for communication; messages had to be sent over land and sea. Traveling from Ludhiana, his hometown, to Delhi in Dadaji's day took as long as it takes to get from Delhi to New York today. It was hard for us to imagine what it could have been like to have the world accelerate and transform so much in one lifetime.

This made it even more amazing when Dadaji asked our opinion about the Internet and the surging stock market and went on to forecast a crash that soon would rattle the economy. He referred to an article he had read in *The Economist* the day before and an editorial in that day's *Times of India*. While many of his contemporaries, or even generations younger than him, convinced themselves that they could not understand or use new technologies, Dadaji had an e-mail account and surfed the

Internet every day. He had studied emerging technologies in depth and had an opinion on the prospects of wireless trends and the pros and cons of DSL versus cable. Dadaji told us how he wished he were just ten years younger so that he could start a new business. By the end of the conversation, we were simply floored by his understanding and knowledge of contemporary trends and ideas. I promised myself that as Sumant and I grew older, we, too, should always be up to speed, never scared of exploring new ways of thinking and continuing to be a force in the world.

When we went home, Dadiji, Sumant's grandmother, had cooked Sumant's favorite foods, and we feasted with delight. Dadaji and Dadiji teased us and laughed with us, telling us stories about their romance. They had renewed their vows a year earlier, after sixty years of marriage. After the ceremony, Dadaji had asked my father-in-law which hotel he had booked them in, so that they could celebrate like any young, newly married couple.

Age, whether it be young or old, is often used as an excuse why we can or cannot do something. But there are great examples of people who break these boundaries every day. How much richer and vibrant would our lives be if we truly felt at every moment that we were capable of anything? We would be there for the ones we love in ways that would offer inspiration, security, and joy. We could create a new paradigm for our children that shows them that they are never too old—or too young—to achieve anything.

53

I promise to teach you
the value of patience.

As a child, I remember feeling so desperate at times about getting something that I had set my heart on. One of the hardest things to learn was the value of patience. I remember my mother telling me this tale one night after I had struggled all day to get something I wanted.

Two monkey friends were wandering around a village near the forest one day when they came across two jars of nuts. The nuts were their absolute favorite, and their eyes opened wide as they got closer to the jars.

The first monkey went running quickly to the jars, not even looking to see if the coast was clear. However, his friend was a bit more careful and cautiously scanned the surroundings before approaching the special treat. By the time he reached the first monkey, however, he could see that his friend was panting with frustration. Desperate for the nuts, the first monkey had put his hand in the jar and grabbed as many nuts as possible. However, his fist was now too large to get his hand out of the small opening. His eyes were full of hunger and lust, and he struggled harder and harder to get his fist out to no avail.

The second monkey watched his friend sweat and pant in frustration. Calmly and slowly, the second monkey approached the second jar, put his hand in, and picked up only one nut with his forefinger and thumb. He easily removed his hand from the jar, ate the delicious nut, and reached in to grab another.

The first monkey watched in frustration as his friend ate nut after nut. However, now even more eager and greedy for the treats, the first monkey could not let go of all the nuts in his fist. He struggled and struggled, but his hand would just not come out. The second monkey was now almost finished with his nuts, and he looked very content and happy.

As the first monkey continued to struggle, his friend jumped as he saw that some of the village women were returning home. The second monkey tapped the first monkey, turned around, and quickly left, leaving several nuts in the almost empty jar. Realizing he had no choice now, the first monkey let go of the nuts, pulled his hand out, and had to leave. He had not even been able to eat one delicious treat.

When the first monkey reached the forest, he was depressed and shaken. He saw his friend in the distance and could not face him because he was so angry about being denied the treats. He started to run in the other direction, but the second monkey caught up with him. The first monkey was about to tell him to leave him alone, when his friend reached out his hand and gave him a nut. The first monkey gratefully looked at his friend and popped the very delicious nut in his mouth.

54

I promise to teach you how to create your own reality.

When we were young, our father taught Gotham and me short phrases to guide us through our daily activities. For us, it was often a game—trying to remember the phrases themselves or adapting them to our own desires and needs. However, now I realize that at a deeper level what he did was build a foundation of spiritual, ethical, and emotional values that have provided us with security in everything that we do.

One of my favorite phrases, which I practiced almost every day, was the following:

I am responsible for what I see.
I choose the feelings I experience.
I set the goals that I achieve.
And everything that seems to happen to me
I ask for and receive as I have asked.

Our father would then ask us to create a list of our desires. Gotham and I developed our own lists, which included things like: I ask for this doll, this Nintendo game, and a weekend with my friends. And then, with the help of our father, we also recited a list that included: I ask for creativity, abundance, knowledge, security, love, and prosperity. To finish it off, we would remind ourselves of our goals, such as to finish a homework assignment, get an A on the social studies test, and make a card for Mom. And then there were the goals our father helped articulate that included treating others with respect, listening, giving, learning, and smiling.

Similar to any other prayer, by reciting these desires and goals every day, we were able to set our intentions for the day, and, as a result, these values permeated our lives. We also were reminded day after day that we create our own experiences, particularly our own feelings. So, if someone criticized us, we remembered that we could only get upset if we allowed him or her to bother us. It was a subtle way to experience the deep truths that no one else could truly hurt us and that what happened around us was a manifestation of our desires. And by stating our goals clearly, we were often able to achieve them. As a result, we saw that we actually had the potential to accomplish anything we decided to pursue.

Even years after Gotham and I stopped reciting this phrase, the lesson was still rooted in our approach to everything we did and saw. Prayers and mantras of empowerment can be powerful tools to shape our children's senses of self-confidence, spirituality, and power.

55

I promise to teach you independence from the judgments of others.

A man once made a journey to a neighboring village with his wife, his child, and his donkey.

The man put his son on the donkey, and he and his wife walked up a hill. As they passed some villagers, the man overheard them commenting, "What a silly man. He makes his wife walk up the hill, when he has such a strong donkey." As they turned the corner, the man immediately beckoned his wife to sit with her son on the donkey.

They soon approached a group of men who were smoking and playing cards. Soon enough the man could hear their snickers. "Poor man. Look at how dominating his wife is. She makes him walk, as she sits like a queen on that poor donkey." Turning the corner, the man took his wife off the donkey and sat upon it himself with his son.

On the street, a group of women were returning from cleaning clothes in the river. As they passed the man, child, and donkey, they looked sympathetically at the woman who was trudging behind them. The man could hear the women huff in anger, "Can you imagine what a brute he his! His wife who has born him a son and who works all day to care for him is forced to walk up such a treacherous hill!" As the family reached the top of the hill, the man told his wife to also get on the donkey, and now his son, his wife, and he weighed it down.

They passed a teacher and some children who were playing in the grass by their school. "Teacher. Teacher. Oh, look!" The children pointed to the donkey. "What a poor animal! He can hardly walk." The teacher glared at the man, turned to her children and said, "Children. An important lesson in life is that we treat all animals with love and compassion. You should never behave like that man."

Exasperated, the man jumped off the donkey, took his wife and child off, and made them walk beside the donkey. When he saw a man approach them, he wanted to turn away but could not do so before the man asked, "Sir, why do you all walk when you have such a lovely donkey. Surely, at least your son could ride on him?"

Throughout our lives, but particularly when we are young, we are very aware of what others think. As a teen, this self-consciousness often reaches its peak, and we carry the baggage of others' opinions throughout our lives. If we could teach our children at a young age to trust themselves and not worry about what others think, perhaps we could save them from some agony down the road. Always worrying about others' opinions creates a never-ending cycle of frustration.

56

I promise to remind you that there are many perspectives to any situation.

When Sumant was two-and-a-half years old, he went for his first expedition with his father. It was a big trip for his dad—the first time he was going to spend several hours completely alone with his baby. He decided to take Sumant to the zoo.

Sumant was so excited when they reached the park. His father bought him a balloon and sat him upon his shoulders, and they went from one animal to the other. They reviewed all the appropriate animal sounds. They pointed out the brilliant colors on the parrots and the lovely feathers on the peacocks. Sumant's father then gave him a wonderful treat; they took a ride on an elephant around the park. It was one of the most special afternoons his father had ever spent.

When they arrived home, Sumant's mother came running out to the car. She grabbed Sumant, giving him hugs and kisses and asking if he had fun. Sumant was licking a lollipop, and he showed his mother the stuffed monkey that his father had bought him. His father beamed with pride, knowing that he had treated his son to an ultimate day of fun and learning. He was excited to hear Sumant's tales of the day.

"Tell Mama all that you saw," his father coaxed.

Sumant beamed with pride and responded, "Rocks, Mama. So many rocks."

57

I promise to help you tap into
your own intuition.

When I became a pregnant, I became obsessed with information, such as what were the right things to eat, the right actions to take, the right thoughts to have, and the right surroundings to establish—all to make sure that my baby developed the right way. I collected books on pregnancy and infancy, surfed online on appropriate Web sites, and joined newsletters that would send me weekly information on the development of my little baby. When I had Tara, my obsession with these books became even more pronounced, and I had a collection of books on my bedside table. I would call my aunt, Amita Aunty, who was a pediatrician, and Gigi, who was the most intuitive mother I knew, about every little question I had about Tara to make sure that I was doing things the right way.

And then one day, I suddenly realized that I was okay. And Tara was okay. We were both doing well. We were on the right path. It was almost a revelation because I had become so lost in the quest for information from authoritative sources that at times I had forgotten to listen to myself. In the end, the information gave me confidence, but it was my intuition, my sense of myself and my child, and my love that made me a good mother. I realized that the right way presented itself to me when I listened to myself and when I looked at Tara and listened to what she was saying, both verbally and nonverbally. I had an innate knowledge about how to be a mother, a knowledge that came from somewhere much deeper than books, articles, and other people's experiences. This insight became a turning point in my journey as a parent; it gave me the confidence to balance all the facts in my head with the flow of love and nurturing that being with my daughter unleashed.

This has been an important lesson for me that has gone beyond the sphere of parenting. I realize now that there is a balance between information and experiential, intuitive knowledge. Facts and information teach us about how things have worked in the past and guide us to avoid mistakes in the future. But there is so much more to any endeavor than the superficial numbers, dates, formulas, and words. Ultimate success comes from experiencing and listening to what our hearts, our environments, our spirits, and those that we trust are saying to us. Freedom from what others dictate is right and wrong and their opinions on what works and what doesn't gives us wings to fly and experience life in a whole new way.

Reflection

WRITE DOWN A STORY about a time when you made an important decision by following your heart. How did this make you feel? Was it the right decision?

58

I promise to empower you to achieve great things.

Once a great, strong lion was lounging about the plains. It was a warm day, and the lion was enjoying the sun above him. Suddenly, the lion felt something scamper along his arm, and with a snap of his paw, he grabbed a small mouse between his claws.

As the lion licked his sharp teeth, the mouse trembled with fear. Before the lion could actually put the mouse in his mouth, he heard a high-pitched squeak.

"Great lord. Most noble king of all animals. Please spare me. I was rushing home to my family. Please do not eat me, and have mercy on such a small creature. I promise that in return I will come help you in a time of need."

The lion laughed at the mouse. "How could such a tiny creature as you ever help me, the greatest animal in the kingdom?" the lion asked. "Don't be so arrogant!"

"Nevertheless," he continued, "I have just finished a good meal and am not hungry. I will let you go today. Now scamper off!"

Relieved, the mouse scuttled away.

A few weeks later, the lion was wandering in a bush when he stepped onto a trap and was jolted up into a net. The lion struggled here and there, but despite his valiant effort, he seemed doomed. As king of the jungle, the lion knew that there was no greater prize than a lion like himself, and he despaired at the thought of becoming a trophy for some boastful hunter. Becoming more desperate by the minute, the lion struggled and writhed but found that he was just getting more tangled and trapped in the net.

Just as he was about to give up, the lion saw a mouse scuttling below him. In seconds, the mouse was nibbling away at the net, loosening one string at a time. Slowly, as one strand released to another, the hole in the net became larger and larger. Soon enough, the hole gave in to the lion's great weight, and the lion was free.

This classic Aesop fable teaches us that we can all find our own unique ways to accomplish great feats. It is important that, as parents, we nurture a confidence in our children that gives them the inner strength, wisdom, and power to achieve anything.

59

I promise to show you that sometimes the most special friendships are found with the most unlikely people in the most unlikely places.

When I was sixteen years old, I spent a summer in the Dominican Republic as a volunteer with a program called Amigos de las Américas. The program's intention is to help foster leadership roles for young people to promote health, education, and community development.

During the orientation that took place in Texas, I remember questioning why I had signed up for this program. As a young idealist, I thought that I could only understand issues of poverty, public health, and education if I immersed myself with the people and cultures that we discussed in the classroom.

I encountered a different sort of mentality when I arrived in Texas. Orientation was more about partying and flirting with a group of new people than about contemplating the greater issues facing the world. As a shy, introverted, serious Indian girl, it was difficult for me to party with the others, and I found myself more comfortable reading a book in my room, feeling awkward about how I didn't fit in. I remember noting one particularly intimidating individual from the group, a loud girl named Lisa who was about six feet tall and the ringleader of the party gang.

Of course, when our groups were announced, I found that I was being sent to a small village called Los Guantes, with the one person I had prayed not to be partnered with—Lisa! I was so perturbed that I considered going straight back home, thinking that there was no way I could spend eight weeks in a remote village with this girl.

The small village, which is about one hour from Santo Domingo, was inaccessible by car, and we had to walk across a shattered, old bridge over a river to get there. It seemed safer to just wade or swim in the water.

Much to my relief, Lisa and I were partnered with different families for our living accommodations. All of the houses in our village were made of tin shacks with patched roofs. I was in a shack with a young couple and their three little girls, Pereira, Leleila, and Vanessa. The cooking was done outside over a handmade oven lit by fresh wood. We bathed in the river, and we were sent out into the fields to go to the bathroom. Our assignment was to help build latrines for the village.

I acclimated to life in Los Guantes in one day. The family was beautiful in every sense of the word, and the children brought me so much joy and freedom. My first morning, I was awakened at dawn by the three girls, along with a host of chickens, goats, and dogs. I helped the mother cook beans, rice, and plantains, which was my meal for lunch and dinner for the next two months. Siestas were a part of the daily routine, and evenings were spent chatting, singing, and dancing. It was a simple and carefree lifestyle, and all of my sixteen-year-old stresses, ideologies, and convictions suddenly seemed irrelevant.

It took much longer to build a bridge with Lisa. But as we began working on our latrines, slowly we started to talk more and more. Lisa was, in fact, as different from me as could be imagined. She had grown up in a trailer park in Nebraska with her father who was an alcoholic. She had been "encouraged" by her aunt to join Amigos for the summer because of her wayward habits with drugs, alcohol, and running into trouble with the local police. Lisa's aunt felt that the exposure would do Lisa good, and she had coordinated the whole trip on Lisa's behalf. Every day, Lisa and I would talk a little bit more, and she admitted that she was disappointed when she heard that I would be her partner because I seemed so quiet and serious. We slowly realized through our conversations, though, that despite our drastic differences, we actually enjoyed each other's company, learning from each other about a life that was so different from our own.

One afternoon, Lisa and I were trying to transport cement from one end of the village to another. It was a hot day, and we had about three bags of cement and one horse. We tried to tie the bags of cement onto the horse, but the bags kept falling off. We then decided that perhaps we could both ride the horse and carry the cement on our laps as we rode. As we tried to maneuver this way and that, we finally ended up facing each other on the horse. We were laughing and crying so hard at the absurdity of our situation. Here we were, two young women with little in common, struggling to carry cement on a poor horse so that we could build a latrine in a small village that was hidden across a river! It was one of the warmest, most memorable, and important encounters of my life, and I knew then that my purpose for coming to Los Guantes that summer was to discover the miracle of friendship.

60

I promise to learn from your faith and innocence that good things are bound to come.

My brother, Gotham, served as a war correspondent for a news channel for more than five years. He traveled to the most conflicted parts of the world, including Afghanistan, Chechnya, Colombia, Sri Lanka, Pakistan, and China. When Gotham returned from his adventures, the most poignant stories were always the ones about the daily struggles of the children. Wherever you find them, children are innocent and curious, playful and joyous. In war, children are the most affected by the violence, hatred, and confusion that surrounds them, because they know in their hearts that this should not be the norm.

During one trip to Chechnya, Gotham was reporting outside a building that had been bombed the night before, when a ten-year-old girl walked by him. As the girl passed, she dropped one of the many tattered books she was carrying in her little arms. Gotham bent down to pick up the book, and he was taken by the look of determination on the girl's face.

"Where are you going?" Gotham asked her, having noted that few children wandered the violent streets by themselves.

"To school," she replied.

It took a second for Gotham to remember that there were no schools open in the neighborhood. Because of the violence, parents were frightened about sending their children out and schooled them at home or in small groups with their friends. Plus, this war-torn area could not afford the risks attached to gathering their precious children in one location.

Gotham watched the girl scurry along, and he decided to follow her, thinking there may be a story in the girl's simple proclamation. After about ten minutes, Gotham watched as the girl entered an abandoned park and sat under an old tree. She opened up her books, took out a piece of paper and a pencil, and began her work.

Gotham approached the young girl and asked her if she was expecting anyone else. Was this her school? Who taught her? What was she studying? As Gotham squatted next to the girl, he saw that her books were not necessarily schoolbooks, but instead they ranged from novels to picture books to magazines.

The girl confidently looked back at Gotham and replied, "This is my school. It hasn't officially opened, and we haven't found a teacher yet. But all that is to come. And when the school does open, I will be here waiting. And I will be ready." She proudly pointed to her books, her letters in her little notebook, the destroyed playground, and her protective tree.

For just one instant, Gotham also saw her beautiful school, her joyous playground, a tree house in the tree, and laughing children and loving teachers running around her.

Reflection

THINK ABOUT AN IMPORTANT event in your life that taught you an invaluable lesson. Write a promise about sharing this lesson with your child.

Love

Cherishing the joy you bring to my life

61

I promise to protect you
with every fiber of my being.

In the aftermath of a devastating fire in Yellowstone National Park, forest rangers went in to assess the damage. The land had been totally decimated. Mounds of ash covered the forest ground; charred, skeletal trees barely stood; and the air was thick with smoke.

As a forest ranger solemnly embraced the awe-inspiring power of nature to both create and destroy, he saw a burnt bird leaning against a charred tree amidst the rubble. Hidden beneath a fallen branch of a tree, the bird's fragile body had been scorched by the rampant fire and smoke. Swept by empathy, the forest ranger had an impulsive desire to bury the innocent creature.

When the forest ranger picked up the bird, it took a moment for him to realize the sanctity of what he saw beneath the bird's wings. Three little chicks came prancing out from under their mother's wings—unaware of the death and desolation that surrounded them. They pecked at each other, chirped their little tunes, and danced around each other.

Their mother, in an effort to protect her chicks from what she instinctively knew would be a life-threatening fire, had taken them to a protective space and covered them with her wings. As the fires raged around her, the mother bird stood—stoic, unmoving, and steadfast. It would have been easy for the mother bird to fly away to safety, but instead she did not move. There was no sacrifice too great to protect her little babies.

"He will cover you with his feathers,
and under his wings you will find refuge."

Psalms 91:4

62

I promise to always remember
the first moment that I realized I was a mother.

I will never forget the first moment that I actually looked at Tara. I had seen her, of course, right after the long delivery. I had held her for a moment then, before she was whisked off to check her vital signs.

I had held her later the day she was born, but I was exhausted from the Cesarean section, from the chaos of the family and hospital staff looking over my shoulders, and from the heavy drugs that put me into a daze. To be honest, I felt overwhelmed, tired, and confused. Despite all the planning and anticipation, I had not really understood what it would mean to have a baby in our lives.

It was not until a day after Tara was born that I really saw and beheld the miracle that she was for the first time. I suddenly was rapt by every tiny part of her precious body. I counted her ten tiny toes and long fingers. I stroked her head of dark black hair. I felt her skin, so soft and pure and perfect. I traced her little nose and rose pink lips.

And when I looked into Tara's dark eyes, I felt as if I could actually see her soul; her unique presence gazed up at me with wonder. I could not help but smile and cry, and a wave of emotion and unbounded love wrapped around my spirit. This was my baby. My daughter. The most precious and miraculous gift I had ever received.

I was now a mother to this innocent, vulnerable, and real little being. I was actually her mother. My eyes swelled with tears, and my heart pounded with a calm joy.

I beheld my little daughter, held her close to me, smelled her baby scent, felt her soft baby skin, and gently kissed her.

Reflection

WRITE DOWN YOUR MEMORIES of the first moment that you saw your baby, so that you can share those memories with your child.

63

I promise to always remember that my love for you is the light that guides me along motherhood's journey.

When I first got pregnant, I was absolutely thrilled. I have always loved children—for their innocence and joy, honesty and playfulness. Sumant and I had waited five years to have a baby, and when I did get pregnant, I knew that this was what I wanted most in the world.

Or so I thought. It was that first night after I realized that we were going to have a baby that fear and anticipation began to creep into my dreams. I found that I was suddenly insecure about everything in my life—my relationships, my maturity, and my abilities. Was I ready to be a mother? Did I actually know what it meant to be a parent? Could I handle all the responsibilities and pressures of raising a child in a world of confusion and chaos?

I was plagued by these questions throughout my pregnancy. At times, I was self-conscious about my nervousness, not even able to admit to Sumant how nervous I was. For wasn't I the one who had been yearning for a child for so long? Yet as my due date approached, along with the excitement came more and more fearful anticipation. I knew our life was going to change in a way we could not even imagine, and I prayed that I would be able to handle it.

Of course, when Tara arrived, in one moment she unleashed a flood of joy, passion, and love that had been nurtured during my entire life. I looked at her and knew that she was exactly what was meant to be. Holding her in my arms, I finally felt a sense of relief.

However, the fears soon surfaced again. It was first the thought of leaving the hospital and going home where there would be no nurses to help manage her. Then it was the anticipation of my mom (who took care of me and Tara for the first three months) returning to her normal life. And it continues to this day when Tara is more than two years old, and I am pregnant again, imagining if I will be able to handle two children.

I realize now that my insecurities creep up when I have the time to think, to be rational, and to envision all the possibilities of the future. But the truth always reveals itself when I let go of all the thoughts, and just be with my child. I hug and kiss her. We talk. We read books. We cuddle while falling asleep. In sharing those quiet, magical moments together, I realize that my love for her will help me through all the questionable moments. Love overshadows all rationality and irrationality. Love presents a window into a world where I am free, where I am secure, and where I can be the mother that I have always dreamt about being.

64

I promise to always remember how your happiness makes my heart pound with utter joy.

From the age of six months, Tara loved to go on the carousel. It was her absolute favorite thing to do, and it was an activity she began to associate with my parents, who would take her to visit the play horses. As Tara got older, she would get more specific about which horse she wanted to ride on. She always wanted someone by her side as she went round and round, bouncing to the music, waving to bystanders, and watching the lights that flashed on and off.

When Tara was just over two years old, Sumant and I decided to take her to ride a real horse at the local Sunday farmers' market. With about six small ponies, the attraction was a hit with young kids, who were led ten times around a small, enclosed circle. As Sumant and I approached the front of the line, we planned for one of us to walk by Tara's side, holding her hand and making sure she did not get nervous.

When we reached the front of the line, we were told that the kids had to go to the horses alone, and no parents were allowed to escort them. Sumant and I looked at each other, nervous to hand Tara off, but at this point she was so excited that we really couldn't turn back. As Sumant gave Tara to the woman in charge, there was a moment of panic in Tara's eyes, but immediately the woman distracted Tara by asking her which horse she would like to ride. Tara pointed to a brown one, and the woman told her that horse was named Champion. As the woman put Tara on the horse, she told Tara to put her hands up in the air so she could put the harness around her lap. Tara put her hands up, keeping them up there long after the woman had fastened her and left. Immediately, Sumant and I jumped, telling Tara that now she could put her hands down and hold onto the saddle so she wouldn't fall. We both looked at each other and laughed, realizing how overprotective we were being!

Tara stroked and smiled at Champion. Sumant and I stood on the outside of the small fence and waved at her. Her smile just took our breath away. She was so happy, so proud, beaming from ear to ear. As the horses began to trot in a circle, Tara sat with her head high, focused on the space in front of her. Sumant and I called Tara's name, and when she spotted us, she would smile or wave. After one or two rounds, Tara became more confident, holding the saddle with one hand and stroking Champion's mane. She looked around, found me and said, "Mama, I love my horsie, Champion." She then saw Sumant, and said, "Papa, I love you so much!" My heart skipped a beat, and in that moment I felt a sense of genuine joy. I looked over at Sumant and could see that he was also completely taken in the moment. He had the most beautiful expression of love on his face, and he blew Tara a kiss, saying, "Baby, I love you, too. I am so proud of you."

As Tara's ride on the horse came to an end, I do not know if Tara, Sumant, or I were beaming more.

Our children have the ability to unleash unexpected moments of unbounded love and ecstasy in our hearts. Such moments are the ones that open our eyes to the magic, miracles, and divinity that love can bring to our lives.

Reflection

REMEMBER A TIME with your child during which you felt complete, uninhibited joy.

65

I promise to love you, with no limits, from the depths of my soul, even when I know that it makes me more vulnerable than I have ever felt before.

Since having children, a wave of unbounded love has flowed from my heart. It is a kind of love I have never experienced before—a love that has no expectations, that feels pure and innocent, and that is willing to sacrifice anything and everything for my babies. It is a love that is so intense that it has made me feel more vulnerable than I have ever felt before.

I think about parents who must deal with children who face illnesses, who are unable to shield their kids from pain or suffering. Now that I am a parent, I can relate, in a way that I never could before, to the feverish desperation that parents have when wanting to protect their children. Unlike with other people in my life, where I can build barriers to protect myself, the love for my children has no barriers, no boundaries.

A few days before Tara's first birthday, we received a call from my aunt that my cousin, Rishi, had a seizure and was admitted into the hospital. He had spent the night getting tests, and our family members in Boston were all in the hospital with him, awaiting the results. My father, being a doctor, immediately knew from the initial symptoms and the kinds of tests that the prognosis would not be good. He booked a flight to Boston right away, and it was a moment like no other in my life, where I felt a true sense of dread.

The MRI of Rishi's brain showed a tumor that consumed seventy percent of the left side of his brain. He was later diagnosed with a brain lymphoma, a serious form of brain cancer. Just two weeks earlier, Rishi had turned twenty. He was a sophomore in college, immersed in all the things that a person who is at the cusp of adulthood would be busy doing. In the ensuing year, Rishi embarked on a painful journey of chemotherapy and radiation that, in addition to getting rid of the tumor, also resulted in the loss of his sight and hearing.

While all of us went through our individual struggles to accept Rishi's illness, I can never forget the agony that my aunt and uncle faced as they watched Rishi suffer. They were, and continue to be, by Rishi's side for every moment of the ordeal. They managed the logistics of sickness and recovery, the doctors, the insurance hassles, and the medication timetables. When Rishi had to leave school and move home, my aunt and uncle made the transition seamless, and they changed their lives to accommodate his every need and desire. They were there to hold him, talk to him, and comfort him in those dark moments when he had time to think, to be still, and to soak in all that had happened. My aunt and uncle did not complain about the exhaustion or what they were going through; they were focused solely on their baby and taking care of him, doing whatever they could to help him. But my aunt and uncle suffered deeply in silence because they had to watch their child suffer, and they could not prevent that.

While all of us assumed he was still almost a child, Rishi proved to be the strongest, most able, and most solid presence in the midst of this trauma. He did not feel sorry for himself, but rather he put his energy into healing and overcoming the challenges that would pile on day by day. Even now, with the handicaps of almost complete blindness and deafness, Rishi is focused on communicating in new ways and on what needs to be done to heal. Rishi has taught us all so much about life and about appreciating the relationships and opportunities before us. He teaches us about belief, faith, and true, unwavering love.

Rishi's illness came at an interesting time in my life—a time when I was discovering the emotions of being a parent. I hurt so much, not only for him, but for his parents because I could relate to their undying commitment to their child. In many ways, Rishi's illness instilled a fear in me about the intensity of my love for my children and the understanding of how vulnerable that kind of love has made me.

But Rishi also showed us that there is nothing as rewarding as loving someone with the kind of abandon that a child inspires. It is the kind of love that touches your very soul, which makes your life rich, vibrant, and full. And it is the kind of love that nurtures those on whom it is bestowed, making them the strong heroes and angels who will teach us lessons and give us the most precious moments of our entire lives.

66

I promise to always remember the tenderness you have awakened in me.

Those first few days of breastfeeding after Tara was born were a real challenge for me. I was exhausted, frustrated, in pain, and depressed that Tara would not latch on with ease. But Sumant sat with me, softly and gently pushing me to keep on trying.

One night, after struggling all day to get Tara to latch on and find the right position to hold her, Tara finally did begin to feed. Despite all the frustration, I was still awed every time she fed, just thinking about how amazing nature and our bodies are. As Tara fed, I settled down, stroked her soft hair in silence, and watched her beautiful face that was so peaceful and innocent.

When Tara was done, she slowly unlatched from my breast. Her eyes were closed, her tummy was full, and she seemed asleep. Tara moved her head here and there, nuzzling close to me. She readjusted herself several times until she was just over my heart. There she settled, falling into a deep sleep to the rhythm of my heart. Her pink lips still puckered a bit, and she placed one tiny hand on my chest. Tara was at home, secure, and in peace, listening to my heartbeat and my soft breath and feeling my skin and the warmth of my body. It was a moment in which I understood complete trust, peace, love, and tenderness.

Afraid to move, I quietly got Sumant's attention, and we both gazed at our beautiful little daughter. We had never beheld something so gentle and beautiful in our lives.

As parents, we feel the complete trust our children put in us. Let us try to never betray that pure and divine emotion. Such trust builds their senses of security and confidence that nurtures and strengthens all of their future relationships.

67

I promise to show you the healing power of love.

Scarlet the cat made headlines in New York City and throughout the world several years ago. Scarlet was a homeless alley cat who lived in an abandoned warehouse in Brooklyn, New York, with her five newborn kittens.

One cold March morning, Scarlet smelled smoke inside the warehouse. Instinctively, she immediately began to save her kittens from the rapidly growing flames, one kitten at a time. Despite the fire getting wilder by the minute, Scarlet did not hesitate one instant before heading back into the scorching flames to rescue the next kitten. Then Scarlet carried them one by one across the street, until she was discovered and rescued by a valiant firefighter and taken to an animal shelter.

Scarlet's eyes were blistered shut, she had massive burns, and her skin was singed. But despite being barely able to stand or breathe, Scarlet continued to cuddle and lick her kittens in the aftermath of her daring rescue. In turn, her kittens stayed near her, licking their mama and giving her the warmth and love that helped her to heal. Three months after the horrible accident, Scarlet and her kittens were well on their way to recovery.

Scarlet showed us how love gives us power and strength to overcome the most challenging situations. She taught us that love gives us reason to persevere. We can depend on it to heal our deepest wounds.

68

I promise to show you
how loving acts last a lifetime.

Sumant's great-grandfather—his grandmother's father—decided at the age of fifty to leave his family and travel to the Himalayas to explore his own spirituality. In the Hindu tradition, this was considered a natural stage in a man's life. He left behind eight children, ranging from twelve to twenty-five years old.

Sumant's grandmother was the eldest in the family, and she was the only one married at the time. Her husband, whom Sumant called Bhara Papa, took on the patriarchal role for all of his wife's brothers and sisters. He paid for their educations, arranged their marriages, and secured their first jobs. The family was forever grateful to him, and for his entire lifetime they gave him respect in word and deed for guiding them.

The youngest of the siblings, Kuku Uncle, was about the same age as Bhara Papa's children. Bhara Papa, therefore, became a surrogate father to Kuku Uncle through his teens and young adult life.

One thing that Kuku Uncle loved more than anything else was to swim. So several times a week, Bhara Papa would put Kuku Uncle on the back of his scooter and brave the traffic of Delhi to take him to a pool on the opposite end of the city for swimming lessons. Bhara Papa took great pride in watching Kuku Uncle race across the pool and was by his side in every swimming competition that he competed in. Kuku Uncle started to collect many trophies, all of which he gave to Bhara Papa, his mentor, companion, and inspiration.

Kuku Uncle went on to medical school and moved to the United States, where he settled down with his wife and kids. When Kuku Uncle retired, he decided to take up his favorite pastime once again—swimming. He joined senior swimming competitions and, to his delight, found that the strokes came back easily, and he began winning many of the competitions. Before every competition, Kuku Uncle prayed and thanked Bhara Papa once again for his support in those early years.

Soon after Kuku Uncle began swimming again, Bhara Papa fell fatally ill, and we all knew that it was just a matter of time before he left us. Kuku Uncle decided that he needed to make a pilgrimage back to India to pay his last respects to Bhara Papa. He packed his clothes and got ready for the emotional journey to say goodbye to the man he had always thought of as his father.

Most important, Kuku Uncle packed all of the swimming trophies that he had won in the last few years. It was time to give this new batch of awards to the man who had nurtured a love and passion in him that had lasted a lifetime.

69

I promise to teach you to trust divine guidance.

Psyche, the most beautiful mortal in the world, was married to Cupid, the god of love, but she did not know it. He would meet her only at night, and he had made her promise to never look upon him for then he would have to disappear. One night, however, Psyche could not resist the temptation to see her beloved's face, and she looked upon him in all his divine glory while he was sleeping. When the wax on Psyche's candle accidentally fell on Cupid's shoulder, he woke up and had to leave the woman he loved. It was against divine law for a god to marry a mere mortal.

Psyche was distraught and decided to dedicate the rest of her days to finding her husband. She guessed that he would be at his mother's home, and thus she fearfully approached Venus, the goddess of beauty. Venus hated Psyche because it was said on earth that Psyche's beauty outshone the goddess's, and Venus had lost many of her worshippers because of this mortal. In her quest for love, though, Psyche set aside any competitive and fearful feelings and begged her husband's mother to let her see him again. Psyche offered to serve as Venus's slave for her remaining days, if only to be able to see Cupid once again.

Out of vengeance, Venus decided to make Psyche attempt virtually impossible tasks to prove her love for Cupid. The first task was to separate a basket full of the smallest seeds of wheat, millet, and poppy before nightfall. If Psyche could not do it, she would face Venus's unrelenting anger. It was an impossible task, but nonetheless, Psyche began. As she laboriously picked out each tiny seed, an army of ants observed her and felt sympathy for the lovelorn girl. The ants marched into the basket and began to separate the seeds into organized piles. When Venus returned that night, she could not believe her eyes. The task had been completed.

The next day, Venus decided to send Psyche on a dangerous adventure to retrieve the golden wool from a special, dangerous breed of sheep. Venus knew that the sheep would attack anyone who came near them, and Psyche trembled in fear as she approached the bushes where they pastured. Desperate, Psyche decided that she would approach them even if she got killed. However, just then, she heard a reed call out to her. The reed told her that if she waited until dusk, when the sheep left the bushes to rest by the water, she would be able to go into the thicket and find plenty of wool on the twigs. This is what Psyche did, surprising her mother-in-law once again.

The next adventure required Psyche to retrieve magical black water from the source of a waterfall that spouted from high in the skies. It was impossible for any human to reach such a height, but once again Psyche found a savior. This time, an eagle who saw her tripping up a mountainside took her flask and flew up to the source of the water.

Thus, Psyche valiantly conquered each task with the help of the elements and animals that wanted to see her happy. Cupid finally became aware of Psyche's longing and realized that he could love no other like he loved Psyche. He took matters in his own hands and flew to Olympus, the capital of the gods, and went to Jupiter, the father of the gods, to beg for his help. Jupiter could not deny the feelings of the two lovers and formally declared

Psyche to be the goddess of the soul, giving her the ambrosia that offered everlasting life.

Thus, through divine intervention and the support of nature, Cupid and Psyche—love and the soul—were joined in matrimony for the rest of eternity.

The ultimate goal of love in most wisdom traditions is to get a taste of the divine. Love opens up a window to God, to peace, and to pure bliss. Falling in love, whether it be with our children or a partner, is the most emotional and rich journey we will take in our lives.

POEM OF MIRABAI

If by bathing daily God could be realized
Sooner would I be a whale in the deep;
If by eating roots and fruits He could be known
Gladly would I choose the form of a goat;
If the counting of rosaries uncovered Him
I would say my prayers on mammoth beads;
If bowing before stone images unveiled Him
A flinty mountain I would humbly worship;
If by drinking milk the Lord could be imbibed
Many calves and children would know Him;
If abandoning one's wife could summon God
Would not thousands become eunuchs?
Mirabai knows that to find the Divine One
The only indispensable is Love.

70

I promise to show you the power
that love has to change the world.

After my grandfather died, my uncle, Chota Papa, shared a story with my family about a memory he had about his mother and father.

My grandfather was a doctor in the army, and so his family—my grandmother, father, and Chota Papa—was stationed in new villages or cities every few years. At one point, they moved to a remote village in India where Western medical care was rare.

Within days of their arrival, word had spread about the miracles that my grandfather was manifesting. From giving simple medications and shots to villagers who had never been exposed to Western medicine to performing surgery and treating common ailments, my grandfather was saving the lives of hundreds every day. Crowds and crowds of people—rich and poor, young and old—would wait outside his one-room office, having traveled hundreds of miles by foot, bullock cart, motorcycle, bus, or car to see him. Despite working for more than fourteen hours a day, there were only so many patients that Daddy could see in one day, and often people would wait for days. But they truly believed that this great doctor would heal them, and thus they would wait patiently to meet this renowned man. Daddy was always smiling and gentle with everyone, and his presence itself began to heal and nurture them.

There were many people who came to visit my grandfather who were poor, hungry, and barely had enough to survive. Chota Papa told about how my grandfather would never charge these patients, but he would still treat them with the same dignity, grace, and compassion as he would the richest man in the city. He would spend the same amount of time with them, and he would spare them no medicine, even if he had to pay for it out of his own pocket. My grandmother would feed the people while they waited and again before they departed, and she would even give them money to take proper transportation home rather than walk in their afflicted state.

After three years, Daddy received a notice that he was to be transferred to a new village. Chota Papa recalls heading to the train station to depart. He describes a sea of people who had come to pay their respects to my grandmother and grandfather and to say goodbye. The railways staff literally had to cordon off the crowds, who were so emotional about his departure. Daddy had touched and saved so many lives that thousands stood outside the train, wanting one last look at their hero before he left them. He was a healer who had transformed an entire village's perception of life, compassion, and charity.

Reflection

THINK ABOUT LOVING ACTS that you and your child can offer your community.

Purpose

Fulfilling your dharma (purpose in life)

71

I promise to always remember the sense of purpose and confidence you gifted me.

For many years, I struggled with what I wanted to do with my life. I found interesting opportunities and good jobs for my resumé, kept myself busy, and even made it to one of the top business schools in the country. But I was always insecure about my abilities and about whether I had the talent or smarts to do something more ambitious, and I constantly questioned if my routine work was making any difference in my life or the world in general.

We were always taught, growing up, that each one of us has a unique purpose in our lives and that when you are doing something you love, time disappears, you are fulfilled, and you are energized by the energy and dynamism of your purpose. This philosophy, at times, made me very stressed because until recently, I really did not feel like I had a particular purpose in my existence. I felt the burden of doing something important, creative, and inspiring, but in my heart of hearts, I was not confident in my own creativity, inspiration, or power.

It was only once I became a mother that it dawned on me that I had nothing to prove to the rest of the world. Suddenly, I felt that my love for my child was the most important, most real, and most powerful motivation in the world. To nurture, to care, to give, to teach, to share, and to love—these were the most important goals to achieve. I surrendered to the love that my baby opened up in my heart, and suddenly the barriers that I had created for myself over the years began to fall away.

In surrendering to that love, I began to feel creative, inspired, and powerful. For the first time, I felt like expressing myself in a way I had never done before—through words, creative projects, and sharing with others. My work suddenly had meaning and purpose because it was coming from a genuine place of love, giving, and caring.

Reflection

WHAT DO YOU LOVE to do? What is your true passion? Think about how you can empower your child to discover and nurture his or her passions.

72

I promise to teach you that every person
serves a unique and valuable purpose.

There once was a boatman who was taking a famous professor across the bay in his
small boat. The simple boatman had deep respect for the professor, who was known
around the world for his deep insights in philosophy, astronomy, and science. The boatman made every effort to make the boat ride as comfortable as possible. It was a rough
night, however, and the boat swayed from side to side and up and down in the water.

The professor gazed at the beauty of the bay. He felt the rhythm of the water and
said, "When one thinks about how the pull of gravity creates such commotion in the
waters, one marvels at the power of nature. Don't you think so, boatman?"

The boatman had really never thought about waves beyond looking at the skies
and the winds to determine conditions for sailing. He shrugged his shoulders and
smiled somewhat uncomfortably. The professor almost rolled his eyes as he com-
mented, "Surely you must marvel at how the laws of gravity conduct such a symphony of movement?" The boatman silently continued to row the boat, feeling a bit
humiliated about not knowing the laws of gravity.

The professor then pointed up to the vast skies and the bright stars that sparkled
above. "How many light years away do you think the constellation Orion is from us?"

the professor challenged. "Can you tell me how much time it would take for us to reach those stars?"

The boatman looked at him, not really understanding the question. For him the stars helped keep track of direction and time when he was in the vast oceans. He had never thought about stars in any other context before. He shifted uncomfortably as the professor asked, "Have you ever thought about how much of your life has been wasted by not studying the deeper questions in our universe?"

The boatman simply replied, "No, sir." By now he was feeling quite inadequate and also a bit angry. He focused on getting across the bay as quickly as possible.

There was a gust of wind. The professor, who was busy formulating his next challenge for the poor boatman, slipped, and in an instant he fell into the bay.

The professor flailed his arms as he struggled in the water. "Boatman, boatman, help me, I cannot swim!" he cried. The boatman looked down at the struggling professor and shouted, "Surely, professor, you must have learned how to swim. How sad that your life should be wasted in this way!"

The boatman let the professor struggle for just a few seconds more before jumping into the water and dragging him back into the boat to safety. The professor, shivering from the cold, now sat in silence, as they completed their journey across the waters.

An important aspect of the notion of dharma, or purpose in life, is to recognize that each of us has unique talents that we can offer to the world. This Sufi story illustrates the importance of accepting, acknowledging, and celebrating the special gifts that each one of us brings to the world.

73

I promise to help you realize
your full potential.

When I was young, I found a little caterpillar on the windowsill outside my bedroom. Seeking some food and shelter, the caterpillar crawled across the long wooden beam, its attention focused on a group of little red ants that scurried at the other end. The creature then snuggled into the wedge of the window, and I watched as it wrapped itself in a small cocoon. I wondered what it would be like to create a small, warm home for myself, hidden away from the rest of the world.

How vulnerable my little caterpillar seemed. I watched day after day as his little home was blown by the wind, drenched by the rain, and warmed by the sun. I saw a bumblebee whiz around and around and a family of ants march by. I could not help myself from knocking on the window when I saw a woodpecker rest on the beam, its attention focused on my little friend. Day after day, I waited for something to happen.

And then early one morning, just as the sun was rising, I looked out my window and saw the cocoon move ever so slightly in the dawn. Slowly, silently, gently, and dancelike, the carefully-woven threads opened up to the world. With each passing minute, I watched as an exquisite butterfly emerged from its sheltered home. Effortlessly, it stretched its wings, a mosaic of color splashed in the finest shapes and lines, and embraced freedom with one quick flutter.

In an instant, with one quick breath, it was gone.

WOMAN WITH FLOWER

By Naomi Long Madgett

I wouldn't coax the plant if I were you.
Such watchful nurturing may do it harm.
Let the soil rest from so much digging
And wait until it's dry before you water it.
The leaf's inclined to find its own direction;
Give it a chance to seek the sunlight for itself.
Much growth is stunted by too careful prodding,
Too eager tenderness.
The things we love we have to learn to leave alone.

74

I promise to cultivate your passions to help you realize true fulfillment.

As Gotham and I were growing up, our parents placed their highest priority on education. While this included sending us to good schools, it also meant exposing us to great literature, mythology, the arts, history, and traveling—to the extent that their limited budgets would allow. Undoubtedly our parents let us know that it was important to study and get good grades, but they also felt that a holistic education meant experiencing life to its full potential. They wanted us to meet different people; to understand different religions by reading holy texts and visiting churches, synagogues, mosques, and temples; and to visit new places so that we could understand history and culture.

Most important, our parents spent a lot of time listening to us, observing our interests, and cultivating our inherent strengths and passions. Gotham was not as interested in math and science as he was mythology, the history of kings and warriors, and the stories of great heroes. Our parents resisted the temptation to get math and science tutors for Gotham, but rather they cultivated his love of storytelling. They bought him comic books and planned holidays to great forts in India or to the Oracle of Delphi in Greece. They helped Gotham write stories, empowering him to express his creativity and imagination.

When Gotham and I came home with bad grades, our parents would not scold us, but rather delve into why we thought we had not done well. Was it because we were not interested in the topic? Did we prefer to focus on something else? They would challenge us to find new ways of looking at the topic, relating it to some greater purpose or fun activity. If despite all that, we were still not inspired by logarithms or frog anatomy, our parents would let go. In their letting go, Gotham and I developed a sense of confidence in our own interests and talents.

I remember a friend complaining to my father that his son was only interested in music and would not focus on his math homework. After desperate attempts with tutors and after-school sessions, his son had finally refused to attend math classes at all. His father was tempted to deny him his guitar and amplifier until he dedicated himself to two hours of math a day. In contrast, my father advised his friend to let go, suggesting that perhaps his son would discover math through the rhythm of his music. In the end, the young boy became a talented and very successful musician. It was easy for him to hire an accountant to manage his finances.

One of the most effective things we can do as parents is to listen to our children and find ways to foster their unique talents. By giving our children the confidence to embrace their passions, we can help them live more fulfilling lives and also allow them to enrich the world around them.

Reflection

DO YOU SENSE a particular talent in your child? Make a promise to foster this talent and to be responsive to his or her interests and passions as they emerge.

75

I promise to teach you how to create abundance.

In Indian mythology, Lakshmi is the goddess of wealth and good fortune. She is the embodiment of beauty and desired by all the gods. Lakshmi was fickle with her suitors, and she was lover, wife, and consort to many gods. Her behavior teaches us that wealth, too, is considered inconstant and should not be taken for granted. Nonetheless, on Diwali, an Indian holiday, we honored Lakshmi, lighting candles so that she blesses our house and brings wealth and fortune to our family.

Saraswati is the goddess of speech, wisdom, and communication. With her husband, Brahma, she produced the four great Vedas, the treatises of all knowledge, and she is the mother of artists, writers, and musicians. Saraswati represents pure knowledge and wisdom. She requires no festivals or grandeur for her attention and is considered a dispassionate voice in the world.

There is a popular story about a young man who went to a teacher in the woods to learn the secrets of unlimited wealth so that he could use them to help the world. The teacher told him about Lakshmi and Saraswati and explained how both are deeply loved and yearned for by every human being. The teacher then told him an important secret about their true nature. He told the young man that if he pursued and loved Saraswati with all his heart, then Lakshmi would get jealous and vie for his attention by bequeathing him with gifts of wealth and fortune.

Thus, the Hindu wisdom traditions say that we should always pursue knowledge first and wealth will naturally follow. In whatever action or career you choose, it is important that you choose it because of the fulfillment it brings you intellectually, spiritually, and emotionally. Success and wealth will surely be the consequences.

76

I promise to teach you about the seeds of true leadership.

One of my closest friends, Grace Rwaramba, shared the following story with me. Grace had returned to Uganda to visit her mother, who was very sick and dying. Grace knew that it would be the last time she would see her mother, and it was a very emotional trip for the whole family. Grace's mother was a great woman—a mother to twelve children and to an entire community that looked to her for guidance and inspiration. She was the prototypical African matriarch who dominated her environment through her compassion and wisdom.

During this trip home, Grace decided to visit Rwanda, her birthplace, and the country that her mother considered home. Grace decided to return to the village where her mother had been born to pay respects and honor her mother's spirit. When Grace arrived, she was taken aback by the rampant poverty. She was soon surrounded by swarms of children who wanted to touch her. The children who pulled at her dress had deep, understanding eyes, yet they also yearned to sing and dance in the face of all that they were lacking. Their faces, dark and chiseled, were beautiful, but also aged in an unnatural way. Their bodies were hard, bones exposed, the signs of malnourishment apparent in their stunted growth and the way they walked. But despite all their apparent hardships, the children still laughed and played as they jostled to be in a good position to touch Grace, ask her questions, and beg for some money or new toys.

There was one boy who stood out to Grace. He looked like he was twelve. Unlike the other children who played and begged from her, he asked Grace to come to a corner so he could speak to her in private. As she started to follow him, her driver, who was waiting in a car, spotted her and ran to shoo the boy away, like a stray dog that was causing trouble.

Nonetheless, Grace asked him what he wanted and was surprised when he asked for her dress. The other children laughed and made fun of him. Grace joined the laughter, saying it was not possible to take her clothes off in the middle of the village. As she laughed, the boy's eyes filled with tears, and he ran away, humiliated.

The driver pulled Grace away, saying the children were like flies and she should just ignore their requests. But the boy's hurt eyes haunted Grace, and she could not forget the sound of his pleading voice making such a strange request.

Grace asked the driver to follow the alley down which the child had run away. After searching for a while, they saw him hiding in a corner. Grace got out of the car and called him, but he immediately began to run away. She ran after him down the broken street, by now causing a commotion as others saw her chase him. Soon there was a crowd running after the boy, assuming that he had stolen something. As they snatched him up, the young boys in the crowd began to push him around, until Grace stopped them saying that the little boy was her friend.

"Why do you want my dress?" Grace asked the little boy. The entire crowd now jeered at him. Quietly, he asked her once more to give it to him, again instigating a cheer of laughter from the crowd. Grace then took him aside and told him that she could meet him tomorrow at a specific time on the same street corner and give him the dress. His eyes silently thanked her.

The next day, Grace came back to the appointed spot, the dress in a plastic bag. As she approached the spot, she saw the little boy curled in a ball, having dozed off while waiting for her. She asked how long he had been waiting, and he replied that he had never left. He did not have a watch, and he did not want to miss her, so he had stayed in that spot until she returned.

As Grace handed him the dress, he quietly said thank you. Once again, she asked, "Why do you want my dress, little boy?"

Assessing her once again, the little boy replied, "My mother is dying, and I would like to bury her in this beautiful dress. Before she got sick, she looked a lot like you, so I thought this dress would be perfect for her to wear when she goes to heaven."

He told her that his mother had the look that his father had right before he died. They both had AIDS, and he knew his mother would die any day now. Grace, swept with emotion, thought about her own mother and how much she shared with this little boy. She began to cry with total abandon and release.

The little boy now hugged her. "Look, Ma'am, don't cry for my mother. She did so many good things in her life. She produced me. I am the eldest of all her children and so it is up to me to take care of her and my brothers and sisters. Just watch me. I will do it. I can do anything. One day, I will be president and take care of all my people, just like now I take care of my mother and my family."

Grace pulled herself together, bid farewell to the boy, and watched as he trotted along with the plastic bag in his hands. In her heart, she knew that she had met a great boy, a leader who would truly take care of many during his lifetime.

77

I promise to teach you to fight passionately for truth.

When I was in business school, I organized a trip to South Africa, for me and my fellow students to learn more about the country, its people, traditions, and, of course, current and future business opportunities.

While there were many highlights from our trip to South Africa, the most poignant moment for me was visiting Robben Island, the remote prison that held Nelson Mandela for twenty-six years. We were fortunate to be taken to the island by Ahmed Kathrada, a freedom fighter who was sentenced for treason on the same day as President Mandela. Mr. Kathrada, a gentleman in his late seventies, was thirty-six years old when he went to prison, the youngest member convicted in the famous Rivonia trial, and the only person of South Asian descent from the group.

Our tour of the prison was somewhat surreal as he told us firsthand stories about almost three decades in prison, and the shaping of a revolution that changed the face of this dynamic nation. We had all read *A Long Walk to Freedom,* Nelson Mandela's prison memoir, but it was truly remarkable to stroll the grounds of the prison as Mr. Kathrada showed us how they would use scraps of rice paper to write notes for the book in tiny handwriting, and bury the paper in marked holes in rocks, before sneaking them out with released prisoners.

On that sunny day, it was difficult for me to feel the scope of the sacrifice these men made at Robben Island, until Mr. Kathrada talked emotionally about how they missed being around children while in prison. Can you imagine a world without the cries or playful laughter of children? He described the wonderful sensation of holding a child after twenty-three years of being deprived of seeing or hearing them.

The most dramatic moments in our time together came as Mr. Kathrada spoke with conviction and passion about the cause for which he had fought. I got chills down my spine as he talked about the camaraderie between strangers who had united for a cause for which they were willing to sacrifice their entire lives or even to die. The prisoners in Robben Island and the people of South Africa believed with utmost conviction that equality is a human right. They did not let their spirits break over decades of repression and struggle, both inside and outside prison walls. Mr. Kathrada described the evening when his guards announced that they had been released.

"They came and said, 'We have received a fax that you are to be released tomorrow.' Our first question was, 'What is a fax?' We had only seen a television for the first time in 1986."

What was most inspirational about this afternoon, however, was seeing that despite his lifetime of struggle, Mr. Kathrada genuinely did not feel any hatred towards white South Africans or the world that turned its back on their fight for so many years. Kathrada, Nelson Mandela, and other leaders in South Africa, went into power with a philosophy of reconciliation and unity and with the desire to rebuild a ravaged country. Such a vision of justice and forgiveness sings of love, peace, and absolute truth.

78

I promise to help you align
your personal values with your life's pursuits.

When I was twenty-three years old, I decided that I wanted to work in the entertainment industry. After aggressively pursuing a number of positions, I was given a tremendous opportunity to serve as the first representative for MTV in India.

I lived in a hotel in Bombay for several months, and then, because I traveled so much, I decided to move to my grandparent's house in Delhi so I would be around my family. I made regular trips to Singapore, the base for MTV Asia, and I traveled throughout India. I supported all of the other divisions of the company in their Indian efforts, including marketing, production, ad sales, business development, and government relations. The most fun part of the job was visiting all of the nightclubs and concerts in bustling cities like Delhi, Bombay, and Bangalore. It was so glamorous to be able to flash my MTV badge at any club and get free entry. It was an incredible experience in which I had fun and learned a tremendous amount about how to package content, structure deals, and conduct business in general.

But one day, all of my excitement about my job dissipated. I was in a car with some other MTV executives who were visiting India. We had just had some very successful meetings with advertising agencies, and we were planning a celebration dinner at a new restaurant. As we were discussing our success, there was an onslaught of traffic, and our driver veered off into an alley to find a shortcut.

We soon found ourselves in the slums. Housing, if you could call it that, was minimal, and children were playing in mud, naked, with flies swarming around them. Pigs and cows dominated the broken streets. Packs of dogs looked ominous in their search for food. Our animated conversation immediately ceased. The reality of the poverty before us was so depressing that it made us all retreat to our own thoughts of guilt and helplessness. There was complete silence in the car.

Suddenly, one of my associates jumped in his seat, saying, "Whoa! Is that cool or what?" We turned and saw a small stall by the side of the road that had a television hanging from the ceiling. A group of young kids, some naked, others in tattered clothes, all shoeless, were standing or squatting on the ground before the television, watching, their mouths agape. On the screen were American kids, dressed in bikinis, shorts, and miniskirts, grinding away to music. At the bottom right-hand side of the screen, the MTV logo spun around proudly. My colleagues cheered as they saw the logo, and they began hooting with pleasure. What success! Animated conversation began again as they congratulated themselves on a job well done, and the plans for the dinner celebration continued.

I, however, sat in horrified silence. In that moment, it dawned on me the role that I was playing in changing the face of India and the world. I was promoting Beavis and Butthead in India. There was no way to deny it. While I felt it was a social transformation that was bound to happen, I was not proud of it.

I realized that India, the land of great traditions, storytelling, mythology, and spirituality, was being colonized by a different type of invader. This colonizer permeated the very essence of values and identity. Media and entertainment were the weapons of choice; they were the most powerful weapons to date because they were changing the values, the culture, and the goals of an entire civilization. Suddenly, the responsibility of my role in this crusade overwhelmed me.

That evening, I had dinner with my colleagues, celebrating a job well done.

The next morning, I called my boss and turned in my resignation. I decided it was time to move on. It was time to change the world in a way that I truly believed in.

79

I promise to teach you to trust your inherent ability to heal.

A young man was going for a walk when he saw a holy man standing on a riverbank, struggling with a scorpion.

The holy man had waded into the water when he saw that the scorpion had slipped in and was drowning. But as the man reached out to pick up the creature, the scorpion stung his hand, and the holy man had to release him in pain. But the holy man reached into the water once again to pick up the creature that had inflicted such pain on him.

The young man watched the holy man and the scorpion repeat this act several times, and he could not resist interfering with what seemed to be a meaningless and painful exercise. He approached the holy man and said, "Respected sir, can't you see that the scorpion will keep stinging you? There is no point trying to save him."

But as the holy man reached out to pick up the scorpion again and it stung him, he turned to the young man and said, "Dear boy, it is in the nature of the scorpion to sting. It means me no harm. And just as it is in its nature to sting, it is in my nature to save. It is also in my nature to believe that in the end, my pure intention to save him will triumph."

And so the holy man and the scorpion continued their drama, and the young man could not resist watching. And to his surprise, after several more tries, the holy man was able to get the scorpion back on land. Having accomplished his mission, the holy man smiled at the young man and continued on his journey.

A guiding belief of many cultures is that it is our inherent nature to love and to heal. We may get distracted and forget this notion from time to time, but if we truly listen to our hearts and our deepest desires, we cannot deny ourselves of this love. As parents, we truly understand this inherent love when we look into the eyes of our children.

80

I promise to always remember that being your mother is my most important role.

When I think about what kind of mother I would like to be, I have to look only at my own mother as a shining example.

My mother is the embodiment of love, compassion, and caring. She has dedicated her life to nurturing and caring for others—her children, her husband, her parents, her siblings, their children, her extended family, and her friends.

My mother makes sacrifices every day, but she never lets anyone know she is making those sacrifices. She is driven by the love she has for others, and she goes to extreme lengths to quietly make sure that those she loves are taken care of.

My mother's love is patient, enduring, strong, and the most stable force in the lives of those around her. She listens to us, but she never demands that we listen to her. She gives, but she never demands that we give back.

I watch my mother with so much love and pride in her role as a grandmother. She plays, laughs, and sings with her grandchildren. She treats them as individuals who have their own ideas, thoughts, and desires. She talks to them, teaches them about the world, asks them questions, and sits and plays with them for hours. She makes sure that I can rest and work, and she never complains that I ask her for too much.

My mother never feels she has to justify who she is or what she does. She is proud to be a mother.

What my mother understands is that being a mother is the most powerful, feminine, demanding, compassionate, fulfilling, and important occupation in the world.

Reflection

TAKE A MOMENT to think about your role as a mother. What qualities would you like to embrace in this role?

Miracles

Realizing the magic
and mystery of the universe

81

I promise to show you the magic in nature and the infinity of the beyond.

Krishna was a mischievous little boy who was always creating trouble and causing anxiety for his mother. Yet Yashoda loved him with all her heart and found it difficult to scold him for she knew that Krishna was more than a naughty child. He was divinity in disguise, and with each practical joke and game of his was the laughter, lightheartedness, and play of the universe.

One day, Krishna had gone to the beach to play with his brother, Bala, and their friends. They ran about, playing hide and seek and building castles in the sand. While vigorously digging to find some water in the earth below, Krishna was curious and tasted some of the sand on his finger. The hard and crusty texture fascinated him, and he took another taste as his friends watched. Knowing that sand was not good for Krishna's stomach, Bala ran back to the village to tell their mother about what Krishna had done.

When Yashoda reached the beach, Krishna had a guilt-ridden expression on his face. Yashoda asked Krishna if he had eaten the sand, and he shook his head, denying that he had done so. She asked him again and then began to pry his mouth open to take it out. Krishna resisted and tried to run away, but he could not escape her strong hands.

Finally, tired of resisting, Krishna opened his mouth. Yashoda gasped, pulling away from her child. She rubbed her eyes in disbelief and looked once again. Tears rolled down her face because inside of him she beheld the most beautiful sight imaginable.

Yashoda saw rolling hills and jagged cliffs, snowcapped mountains, and a full rainbow reaching out of a waterfall. She saw a purple and orange sunset and the crystal moon shining above a strong, expansive sea. She saw vast lands and skies, flowing rivers, and sand dunes. She saw species of animals from times long past. She saw flocks of birds, a family of lions, herds of zebras and elephants, colonies of snakes and insects, and a wolf howling into the night. She saw flickering lights in an endless dark night sky, shooting stars, and planets far away in distant galaxies. She saw a group of children giggling and playing and castles built in the sand. And then, as Yashoda looked closer, she saw a little boy sitting in the sand with his mouth open. It was little Krishna, and she saw herself kneeling above him.

In that instant, Yashoda fainted. Quietly, Krishna closed his mouth and stroked his mother. He kissed her cheek and gently helped her to sit up as she opened her eyes. In a calm, gentle voice, Krishna told his mother that there was no need to worry. She had glimpsed the divine and had witnessed infinity. He was the mountains and the sky, the water and the wind. He was time immemorial—past, present, and future. He was the vast expanse of consciousness and the solace that lay in the silence of the soul.

Krishna then smiled at his mother, took her hand, and led her home.

82

I promise to remind you
of the many miracles you taught me to see.

Tara has the most amazing smile that I have ever seen. It is a smile that radiates from within, that is confident, yet shy, and that is expressed through her entire body. And with her smile, Tara has the ability to spread joy and happiness to others.

Tara's smile has taught me so many lessons about kindness, giving, and acceptance. She is too young to judge at whom or what she should or should not smile. For Tara, everything and everyone is something to smile about. She smiles at the rain. She smiles at music. She smiles at the dog; in fact, she smiles at the dog's food. Her entire body giggles and shrieks with joy when she sees other children and hears their laughter.

One day, I was buying a newspaper, and there was a homeless man on the sidewalk beside us. To me, he smelled horrible, and his hands and face were black with bruises from some obviously violent mishaps. Holding Tara tightly, I wanted only to buy the paper quickly and leave.

But as I was paying, I could hear Tara making gurgling sounds, leaning toward the man. She was waving her hands and giving him some of the most precious smiles she has ever given. For Tara, he was as special, beautiful, funny, and entertaining as all of the other things she experienced in her life. There was no part of Tara that felt he wasn't deserving of her gift.

The man, now aware that Tara's shrieks were directed at him, looked up in surprise, visibly unnerved by her warm, enthusiastic, playful call. He looked down and then up at Tara again, returning her smile with a peek-a-boo that made her laugh and smile some more. He then looked at me and said, "Please let her know one day that she once gave a hopeless man some hope. She is beautiful. Thank you."

As we walked away, Tara waved goodbye, only to be distracted a moment later by a passing motorcycle. She squealed with excitement as the driver revved the engine and raced on by.

Reflection

THINK ABOUT A LESSON, new emotion, or discovery that you learned from your baby. Promise to share this gift with him or her one day.

83

I promise to foster the magic
of your imagination.

My friend told me about her four-year-old niece, Clarice, who has an imaginary friend named Tommy. Tommy is a little, green leprechaun who is always by Clarice's side. He consults Clarice on important matters and is often the instigator behind Clarice's mischief.

One day at school, Clarice learned that St. Patrick's Day was the following day. She came running home to tell her mother that they had to prepare for Tommy's birthday. Clarice's mother made a decision to indulge her daughter's dreams, and they baked a cake for Tommy. They also planned for a dinner that included all of Tommy's favorite foods, some of which were identical to Clarice's, like pizza and French fries, and others, like green spinach and peas, which Clarice was not necessarily fond of, but which her mother was happy to cook for the special occasion.

The next morning, when Clarice awoke, she found some wonderful surprises. The house was full of green treats, balloons, and streamers; her mother decorated it just for Tommy. In fact, when they went to the bathroom, they found that even the water in the toilet was green, and there was green toothpaste out for Tommy. Clarice smiled from ear to ear, and she told her mother that Tommy was overjoyed. That evening, the entire family sat down for dinner with Tommy, and they had a grand celebration for his birthday. Clarice said it was the best party she had ever been to, and Tommy agreed. Clarice fell asleep with a content smile on her face, entering a world of green leprechauns and celebration.

The story of Clarice and her friend, Tommy, is an inspiring tale for parents on how we can foster our children's imaginations. Clarice's mother supported the magical and wondrous world that Clarice created. Clarice reveled in the excitement of the day, and she would have such special memories of it for years to come. In time, Tommy will probably disappear from Clarice's life, but for the time that he is with her, he gives her vision, creativity, joy, power, and love.

"There's no use trying," Alice said, "one can't believe impossible things."

"I daresay you haven't had enough practice," said the Queen. When I was your age, I always did it for half-an-hour a day. Why, sometimes I've believed as many as six impossible things before breakfast."

-from Through the Looking Glass and What Alice Found There, *by Lewis Carroll, 1872*

Reflection

MAKE A DECISION to visit your child's world every now and then. See the world through your child's eyes, without letting your own voice get in the way. Let your child show you some magic that you never knew was there before.

84

I promise to look at the world
with you with curiosity and wonder.

We take so much for granted in our daily lives that it is important for us to set aside moments when we can look at the world with our children and appreciate its divinity.

The world around us is full of miracles and magic.

Look at a flower. The flower was once a seed, and the seed came from another flower. But for the seed to become a flower it needed the earth, the rain, the sun, the clouds, and the air. To look deeply into the nature of the flower, you would see that it took the whole world to make the flower. And similarly, it takes the whole world to make anything.

Look at an object you have never appreciated before. If you look at a chair, look at it with new eyes. See the wood and imagine the tree from which it came, the wind and sun that nurtured it, and the rains that helped it grow. The chair is also from a carpenter's skilled hand, factories that manufactured it, people who sell furniture, and their families who nurture them, and so on. It takes the whole universe to conspire to create everything that exists.

You and I are also the result of love, mystery, evolution, situations, and circumstances—a symphony of events, chance encounters, dreams, and hopes that conspired to create us. For you and I to exist, thousands of people have lived, loved, and had happy and sad times. The entire history of all of our ancestors is contained in you and me, as is the history of their relationships and the times and places they lived in.

As we look upon each other and the world, let us remember that we are the embodiment of all that has existed, and that we represent the seeds of what will exist in the future. Let us look at the world with such eyes, and we will never cease to experience wonder.

Reflection

LOOK AT AN OBJECT that you use every day and think about all the resources and people that made it a reality. Make a promise to practice this exercise one day with your child.

85

I promise to help you experience miracles so that you can realize your true inner power.

I learned how to fly when I was sixteen. Not to fly an airplane, but to actually fly. It is one of those personal talents I haven't shared with many in the past because people look at you strangely if you discuss your flying style. But flying came quite easily to me, and it is something I can do quite effortlessly.

There are many references to flying in traditions from around the world. In the seventeenth century, St. Joseph of Cupertino was known as a levitating saint in the Christian world. In fact, St. Joseph had a hard time staying on the ground. He would begin to float up in the air and go into an ecstatic state every time he heard any reference to God or holy things. He would cause so much spectacle and embarrassment for his church that for thirty-five years he was not allowed to attend the choir, eat in the refractory, walk in procession, or say Mass in church.

St. Theresa of Avila, a practical and sensible saint from the sixteenth century, also found that she was sometimes lifted into the air involuntarily. It was a bit of a cumbersome experience for her because she was mostly focused on her organizational duties in the church.

To be clear, my flying is more like hopping about here and there than actually floating in the air. Sitting in a cross-legged position while meditating, one repeats a traditional saying and the body reacts by wanting to move upward in a small hop. It is a well-known and somewhat controversial phenomenon that has been documented by the transcendental meditation movement over the past few decades, and it is a common practice described in detail in ancient Indian texts. Theories abound on how and why it happens and the authenticity of the experience.

Learning to fly, or hop, at the age of sixteen actually gave me a sense of confidence and grounding through my teenage years and beyond. Out of meditation, that jolt of energy that pushed me up into the air for that first bounce was a true experience of a miracle. It let me experience the reality that I had the power through my mind and my consciousness to make the impossible possible. It gave me a tickle of bliss and a knowledge that there is so much more to life than what we see or are told is possible.

86

I promise to help you see that assistance comes in many guises.

There once lived an old man who had total faith in God. He believed that God would always be there to guide him and to protect him from all evils.

One summer, the old man's village was beset with a violent storm. It was a storm like no one had witnessed in generations, and the rains pounded the village day and night. Very soon, the villagers began making preparations to evacuate because they anticipated a huge flood. The old man watched everyone panic, pack, and leave town with their children, animals, and precious goods. When the old man's neighbors pleaded with him to leave, he replied, "No worries. I know that God will take care of me."

Very soon, the village was empty. However, the rains had not stopped, and the old man found that the ground floor of his house was flooded. Confident in his belief in God, the old man moved to the second floor. The rains did not stop, and some brave villagers withstood the storm and came to rescue the old man with a boat. The old man, however, once again refused to leave and sent the villagers away. "God will take care of me," he proclaimed to them.

A few days later, the water had risen and the second floor of the house was also flooded. Unnerved, the old man moved to the roof of his house. He watched the rains with awe and marveled at the power of his great God. Soon, the waters started to flood his rooftop. The old man was still not worried because he truly believed that God would save him.

Once again, some villagers braved the storm to come and help the man. This time they arrived in a helicopter and called out to him from the rainy skies to come away with them. Still confident, the old man told them that he would be okay and God would take care of him. Defeated, the villagers departed with tears in their eyes because they knew that the old man would not survive the storm.

The waters rose. The rooftop was overtaken by the flood. And the old man drowned.

As the old man reached heaven's gate, he was very angry. He stood up to God, proclaiming, "How could you let me die! I had complete faith in you, and yet you did not save me."

God smiled gently at the old man and replied, "First, I gave you a warning and sent the villagers to plead with you to leave with them. Then I sent a boat and even a helicopter. What more, dear son, could I have done?"

A valuable lesson for children is to accept that God or spirit is there to support and guide them. This story teaches us all to have faith in God's wisdom. It teaches us that the universe finds ways to help us every day, and assistance is there if only we are willing to embrace it.

87

I promise to help you to embrace
the unknown and not fear the inexplicable.

When I was thirteen, my father brought home an Ouija board. He sat Gotham and me down and asked us if we were interested in getting in touch with other spirits. He explained that there were energy fields around us that we could not touch, see, or hear, but which were as real as gravity. We both weren't so interested in the theory as much as the thought of getting in touch with our dog, Nicholas, who had recently passed away. So when we both enthusiastically replied yes, our father opened up the box, which had a board with the alphabet, YES, and NO on it and a movable piece with a little window that highlighted the letters on the board.

Gotham and I each put one finger on the piece and asked, "Are you there?" We repeated the phrase for a few minutes, and when nothing happened, Gotham started to get bored and wanted to go play a video game instead. But our father encouraged us to keep asking for the spirit and let go of any expectations we had about what would happen. After a few more calls, suddenly the piece began to move. I eyed Gotham, thinking that perhaps he was forcing it to move, but I could see in his nine-year-old eyes that he was also questioning if I was moving it. I realized that neither of us was pushing the piece, but rather our fingers were being guided by something else.

The piece first moved to YES, answering our question, "Are you there?" I then asked the spirit what its name was. Slowly, it spelled its name: N-A-R-I-A-N. I knew for sure then that Gotham was not pushing it because he surely could not have thought that up on his own. Our father, who was simply watching us, leaned forward, fascinated. We began to ask questions of Narian. Where was he from? How long he had been a spirit? Where did he live? And, most important, did he know Nicholas, our dog? Narian had lived in Pakistan in his last life, had passed away fifty years or so ago, and did not reside in one particular area anymore. He enjoyed being free in the vast space of the universe. Most important, though, he told us he knew Nicholas, and he said that is why he had responded to our call. He told us that Nicholas was very happy, which made both Gotham and I sigh with relief.

There are many things in life that we cannot rationally explain, but if we remain open to exploring them, our lives will be more magical and miraculous. Rather than fearing the unknown, we can explore different worlds, peoples, and places with our children and together tap into many of the universe's secrets.

88

I promise to show you
the power of sharing your dreams.

Several years after India gained independence from the British, my grandmother, Maa, decided to take my father and his brother to the Independence Day parade. She knew that Jawaharlal Nehru, India's first Prime Minister, would be there, and she wanted her sons to see the great man who had stood with Mahatma Gandhi to win freedom for India.

Maa bought new clothes for both boys, and spent days deciding which sari she should wear. She wanted her sons to always remember this day, and feel the significance of celebrating their freedom.

They joined millions of people on the streets of Delhi to watch the extravagant parade. Maa stood with pride as she watched the Indian Army, Navy, and Air Force brigades, the police and firefighting forces, and government officials march by. She stood tall knowing that these men and women represented a free India. My father and his brother joined the other children waving flags and balloons and cheering all those who passed.

Suddenly, the cheers became louder and more fervent, and they saw that Mr. Nehru was coming. The noise was deafening, and around them, people were sobbing with joy and excitement. As his car slowly passed where Maa was standing, Mr. Nehru turned. He seemed to look straight into Maa's eyes, and as the car slowly moved on, he plucked the rose from his lapel and threw it to my grandmother. The crowd gasped and stepped back in awe. Maa proudly picked up the rose and held it up for the crowd to see. They applauded.

When Maa arrived home, she emptied a room in the house. In the middle of the room, she placed a table and in a single vase of water, she put the rose. For several weeks people came to the house to look at the rose. When they entered the room in which it was housed, they took their shoes off, tiptoed silently to it, and looked at it with awe, reverence, and wonder. The whole house seemed to be permeated with silence and the presence of spirit. When the rose began to fade, Maa threw a party for her loved ones and as the guests departed she gave each one a faded rose petal.

My father wondered what was so special about those rose petals. "That rose represents the collective soul of India," Maa told him. "In those rose petals were the dreams, the aspirations, and the longings of a suppressed people seeking freedom. And, in those rose petals are our hopes for the future, our passions, our love for each other, and what we strive to become. The rose, my child, is the essence of our soul." For the first time, my father, then an innocent boy of ten, felt a connection with a greater soul and believed in the power that comes from sharing a collective dream.

As parents, we strive to create a world of opportunity, happiness, and freedom for our children. Think of the dreams we would realize if we joined together to scatter rose petals in every corner of the earth.

89

I promise to help you recognize life's miracles.

Giggling to herself, my four-year-old cousin, Ananya, whispered in my ear, "Give him another spoon. He's thirsty. Go on, just give him another spoon."

Colors whirled before my eyes. Arms nudged and poked. Sobs and salutations swirled. Incense tantalized my nose, holy mantras echoed in the distance, and the sunlight reflected against plates of silver and gold that framed the shrine. Baffled, nervous, emotional, and joyful, my hands shook as I made my offering. Silently, amidst the hysteria, I had my moment with God.

Outside, old men and women danced in jubilation. A young sadhu chanted hymns as a hunchbacked beggar woman with a malnourished baby in her arms cried uncontrollably, hailing praises to the sky. A frenzy of voices compared tales and techniques, while a crowd of scientists hypothesized explanations for this bizarre phenomenon that defied common sense. Today was a day of miracles, and even the skeptics had to admit that something magical was in the air.

Ananya took the spoon from my hand and filled it again with milk. Kneeling on the ground, she placed it next to the trunk of the marble statue of the elephant god, Ganesha. The milk, within a minute, disappeared before our eyes. The god literally drank it, sucking it slowly from the spoon. Unaware of the gasps and cries around her, my cousin, innocent and joyful, simply offered another spoonful to the thirsty god.

Later that day, CNN, the BBC, and broadcasters throughout the world announced the bizarre phenomenon that took place over the course of 24 hours in Indian households and temples throughout the world. Reports showed lines of people outside holy shrines, waiting to make their offerings. In fact, all the gods were drinking. A line protruded from the flower shop at a five-star hotel because the small stone statue in the corner of the store was thirsty for milk as well. Headlines the next day read, "Milk Shortage in Delhi Due to Excessive Consumption by the Gods."

To experience a miracle, as it is, may be unique. But to experience it with millions of other people is a gift from God. The day the gods were thirsty in India was a day of celebration and revelation. People danced in the streets, friends and relatives shared their visions, and the elders knowingly and approvingly nodded their heads. Children were dismissed from school early, and shops and restaurants closed. Communities gathered together at places of worship. There was laughter and excitement, and there was a reason to smile. There was a moment when all else ceased to exist, and we were reminded that we live in a world of mystery.

In a world of pollution, violence, crime, poverty, and depression, we sometimes forget that there is magic in our universe. At times, when things look dark and dismal, we need hope. We need reassurance that our faith has some meaning. The "milk miracle" in India gave people a reason to hope, a reason to believe, and a reason to dream of something better. It let us know that something greater, something more meaningful, exists for us.

MIRACLES

By Walt Whitman

Why, who makes much of a miracle?
As to me I know of nothing else but miracles,
Whether I walk the streets of Manhattan,
Or dart my sight over the roofs of houses toward the sky,
Or wade with naked feet along the beach just in the edge of the water,
Or stand under trees in the woods,
Or talk by day with any one I love, or sleep in the bed at night
*   with any one I love,*
Or sit at table at dinner with the rest,
Or look at strangers opposite me riding in the car,
Or watch honey-bees busy around the hive of a summer forenoon,
Or animals feeding in the fields,
Or birds, or the wonderfulness of insects in the air,
Or the wonderfulness of the sundown, or of stars shining
*   so quiet and bright,*
Or the exquisite delicate thin curve of the new moon in spring;
These with the rest, one and all, are to me miracles,
The whole referring, yet each distinct and in its place.

To me every hour of the light and dark is a miracle,
Every cubic inch of space is a miracle,
Every square yard of the surface of the earth is spread with the same,
Every foot of the interior swarms with the same.

To me the sea is a continual miracle,
The fishes that swim—the rocks—the motion of the waves—
       the ships with men in them,
What stranger miracles are there?

90

I promise to show you that where you came from is a long time ago in eternity.

When my mother got pregnant, she discovered that she had an innocuous form of anemia called thalassemia minor. The fascinating part about this discovery was that it is a trait unique to the Mediterranean region of the world. From her blood, it was revealed that our ancestors could be traced back to the time when Alexander the Great conquered North India in 325 BC.

My mother has passed on this blood trait to both Gotham and me. As young kids, we had so much fun creating stories about our wayward ancestor. We imagined a Greek soldier having a passionate affair with a young girl in a village that he passed through during their conquest. Or perhaps he was one of the great artists that Alexander brought to India, who fell in love with a rebellious maiden and then immortalized their love through his art and through his offspring. Or maybe one of Alexander's women was given to an Indian prince in marriage, resulting in this mix of bloods from two different lands. What secrets, what passions, what colorful tales could be imagined from this medical discrepancy!

Each of us carries the memories of the thousands who came before us. It is said the human species dates back 8,000 generations. That indicates two people per generation who came together to create a new life, who in turn created new life, and so on and so on. We are reflections of the loves, wars, hopes, despairs, dreams, and disappointments of familiar ghosts who have lived to make our existence a reality.

I look at my children, and I am awed by the throbbing of life throughout the ages that has made them the beautiful beings who sleep so peacefully in my arms. I think about the colorful history that has brought our family to this stage, and I imagine the great stories that are yet to be told.

Reflection

CREATE A STORYBOOK with your child of your favorite family tales—past, present, and future.

Spirit

Knowing yourself

and your true essence

91

I promise to find moments where you
and I can glimpse pure divinity.

When Sumant and I were living in India, we were invited to join a delegation
of celebrities who had come to Delhi for a conference on children's poverty.
After a fancy dinner at a five-star hotel, we were asked by Rajeev Sethi, one of
India's foremost human rights activists, if we would like to join him for a midnight
Sufi concert at one of the famous mosques in Delhi.

A small group of us—including a prominent American politician, a European
rock singer, a Nobel Peace Prize winner, and a famous economist—headed to the
Nizamuddin mosque. The cars stopped at the entrance of a slum, and Rajeev urged
us to follow him. Dressed in our fancy clothes and high-end shoes, we trudged
through the muddy streets of this township. While I had often visited this area during
the day for shopping, it was somewhat surreal walking through the empty alleys that
were usually full of spice markets, flower vendors, fabric merchants, jewelers, loud
shopkeepers, and aggressive beggars. This night, we saw only some stray animals—
dogs, pigs, and cows—and curious eyes peeking out of shops and makeshift homes.

Rajeev led us through labyrinthine alleys, taking us into the heart of the township. While I had always thought of this area as a slum, I realized as we proceeded

deeper that the centuries-old structures, while looking decrepit, old, and tattered, were actually beautiful inside. With painted walls, intricate carvings, elaborate wooden doors, and traditional crafts inside, they were warm abodes that had hosted generations of families since the thirteenth century. I realized that I was seeing a part of India that I had never ventured into before.

We finally reached the mosque and were greeted by an elderly man dressed in traditional Indian clothes, who motioned to us to sit on the ground of the mausoleum. At this stage, the politician jumped in front, putting out her hand, and in a loud, commanding voice, introduced herself, emphasizing her well-known name. The old man looked blankly at her for a moment, not understanding her point nor recognizing her important name, and smilingly invited her to sit again. As we settled down, the rock singer began to boast to the old man and us about how she had worked with Nasrat Fateh Ali Khan, the world's most famous Sufi singer, before his death. She threw around names of her famous musician friends to the old man who just smiled.

The old man, speaking in Hindi, then introduced his two sons and two grandsons, ages nine and five. As one son began hitting the tabla, a traditional Indian drum, and another son began playing the harmonium, the three generations of men slowly began to sing. Their songs praised their love of Allah, and my heart skipped a beat as I listened to the beauty of their voices. I glanced upward, and I could see the dark eyes of women peering at us from behind a screen. For the next hour, their voices filled the mosque with an exuberant celebration of God, spirit, and life.

When they finished, we all sat in complete silence for about ten minutes, soaking in the power of the experience. We were humbled by the journey that they had gifted us. We had been taken to a place where we did not need to hold on to our identities for security. It did not matter if we were powerful politicians, revered intellectuals, or rock stars. In the presence of divinity, we felt an equality and connection to each other that went beyond the ego.

It is important in life to find moments when we can enjoy spirit. Whether through our religion, meditation, prayer, music and the arts, physical exercise and yoga, or walks in nature, moments when we connect with something deeper help us to realize the magnificence of our world and our existence.

92

I promise to help you experience the bliss that comes when your body, mind, and soul become one.

I started learning traditional Indian dance when I was four years old. Dance was a special way to connect with my Indian heritage while growing up in the United States. Through the stories of the dances, I learned about Indian mythology, gods and goddesses, and the great adventures and traditions that shape our culture. Dance was also a good way to connect with my body, with rhythm and music, and with different forms of expression.

For most of my dancing career, I learned and memorized the steps quite well. I thought I was a relatively good dancer, and I enjoyed the performing aspect. As a quiet and shy person, dance gave me an outlet to express myself with fewer inhibitions. It was so easy to delve into the world of the characters, the eye and neck expressions, and the fast footwork that characterizes Indian dance.

It was during one of my practice sessions, however, that I truly experienced the essence of dance. I was practicing a dance that I had done over and over again for a big, upcoming performance. The dance was a favorite of mine, where Radha, the lover of the God Krishna, is flirting with him. Normally, as the music began, I would envision the first few movements in my mind's eye, calculating the right time to begin.

But this time, when the first notes and beats sang, I found that my mind had drifted to another place. Suddenly, my body began to move in the most free-flowing, seductive, and effortless manner. I suddenly was not there anymore. The dance had taken me over, and I was like a puppet expressing a greater, much grander story. I was the music, the beat, and the intricate footwork. I became Radha, the goddess, and was divine in my expression through my body and my face. I watched Mallika, the body, radiate and expose the goddess. I was in love, in bliss, and totally in spirit.

When the music stopped, it took several minutes before I came out of my inspired state. There really was nothing more to think about or practice at that stage. I had touched something so sacred and special that I just thanked God for such a divine experience.

Reflection

THINK ABOUT AN ACTIVITY that you can teach your child—dance, yoga, martial arts, or a particular sport—that will help him or her build an awareness of his or her body and cultivate the experience of spirit.

93

I promise to teach you that we all experience spirituality in different ways.

After I graduated from college, I spent several months traveling around the world. One of my more "daring" adventures during this whirlwind tour were two weeks that I spent in Southern China by myself.

I arrived in China directly from India, and I was shocked by the contrast between the two countries. In India, religion is reflected in every corner, in clothing, architecture, shops, and music, whereas in China I had not come across any outward signs of such spirituality. Thus as one of my first destinations in China, I decided to visit the Yunnan province and the city of Kunming, an area that hosted numerous temples that had been spared during the Cultural Revolution.

My first morning in Kunming, I pulled out my *Lonely Planet* guide. I located the Yuantong Temple, a Buddhist temple that is more than 1,000 years old, and headed to the bus station. The woman selling tickets did not understand any English, so I pointed to the address in the book, and she read the Chinese characters. She directed me to the appropriate bus, and I began my journey.

After about forty-five minutes, the bus driver said we had arrived, and I got off the bus. I was in for quite a surprise when I walked through the gates. Rather than arriving at a holy temple, I heard blaring music and saw an ocean of Chinese tourists. I had gotten off at the Yunnan Minorities Village, a theme park that showcases Chinese minorities. The temple was nowhere in site. I decided to spend the day at the village and had a good time visiting the small model villages, buying some crafts, and watching song and dance performances.

The next morning, full of renewed energy and commitment, I headed to the bus station again. I took out my book, showed the address to the ticket woman, who sent me to a bus. When I got on, I confirmed with the driver that I was on the correct bus. After forty-five minutes, the bus driver pointed to me and indicated it was time to get off. I saw once again that we were at the Yunnan Minorities Village. "No, I want to go here," I said, pointing once again to my book. The driver aggressively nodded his head and pointed to the gates once again. Frustrated, I pointed to the book again, but he would no longer listen to me. I was at a complete loss about what to do, when a young Chinese man asked me in broken English if he could help.

I explained my predicament, and when he looked at the book he chuckled, saying that the Chinese address in the book was written wrong. Desperate now to visit the temple, I asked the young man to ask the driver how I could get there, and he told me that unfortunately I would have to return to town and take another bus from there. Of course, the bus would not be returning to town for another three hours!

So with no choice, I got off the bus, upset with my book and my inability to communicate, admitting that I did not think I could tolerate another morning at the Village. Almost in tears, I felt a tap on my shoulder, and the young Chinese man asked me, "Would you like to spend the day with my family?"

"My mother, father, grandfather, grandmother, uncle, and aunt," he said, introducing each member of his family, slowly and obviously proud that he was able to remember the right English terms for each individual. Figuring I had nothing else to do, I decided I might as well spend the day with his family.

After visiting a few of the villages, Hunan informed me that it was time to eat lunch. We entered an outdoor dining space that was clamoring with busy conversation and lots of food. Hunan quickly grabbed a table, and before I could even sit down, there were piles of dishes before us.

When we were done with the food, Hunan's grandmother did something that surprised me. She said something to the whole family and everyone put their hands together in prayer and closed their eyes for a moment of silence. In the hum of activity in the food market, this gesture had a major impact on me because it was the first time that I had witnessed anything somewhat spiritual in China.

I could not resist asking Hunan later about the prayer. His English was not so good, but he explained to me that his grandmother always thanked God for every meal because she had gone many years without food. He told me she had spent several years in "work camps" during the Cultural Revolution and that it was God who helped her survive the upheaval in her life. I asked Hunan if they visited a church or temple, and he took a second before saying, "No, there really is no need to."

Carefully, I reexamined his grandmother. I realized that what I had been looking for all this time in China was staring me straight in the face: a quiet and somber, but genuine, spirituality.

I had found what I was looking for in Kunming. The next morning, I packed my bags and left for my next destination.

Reflection

WHAT SPIRITUAL VALUES, what vision of God or the infinite, do you hope to pass on to your child?

94

I promise to teach you
that your spirit never dies.

When Sumant and I got married, we were blessed to have eight of our grand-parents, all of whom were strong and healthy, celebrate our union together. Our grandparents, all in their seventies or eighties, were joyful, vibrant, and full of life. Sumant's grandfather, Bhara Papa, danced so vigorously by jumping up and down that we had to stop him for fear he would overexert himself. Likewise, his grandmother, Dadiji, danced for four hours straight, smiling, beautiful, and happy—an image that we will all hold forever. I remember seeing Sumant's other grand-mother, Naniji, watching me from the corner as I danced with her beloved grandson. My grandmothers, Nani and Maa, best friends with each other, sat together observing and gossiping about the hundreds of guests who were all there in some form because of these two matriarchs. My grandfather, Nana, quietly made sure that everything was running smoothly. In the tradition of our marriage, our four grandfathers joined our families—the Chopras and the Mandals—with warm embraces and proud smiles.

When Tara was born, she was also blessed to have seven of her eight great-grandparents alive. We made early visits to India so that our grandparents could hold their great-granddaughter. I watched with emotion as I saw them marvel and hold Tara, who was so pure, innocent, and joyful. As I watched Nana play games with Tara, I remembered how he had played those same games with me thirty years before. I walked Tara through the ghost-filled rooms where Daddy, my grandfather who passed away before she was born, used to sleep. I knew he was there with us, as we blew a kiss to his picture on the mantel.

Since then, I have given birth to Leela, our second child, and we have lost two more grandparents. It is strange to watch the passing of one generation as a new generation comes in. These little beings reflect the faces and moods of an older generation. I have always seen Daddy's tenderness and caring in Tara. Her eyes show the deep compassion and love that he extended to everyone around him. Her meticulousness to details and order is an echo from my Nana. When I watch Tara dance, jumping up and down to Bollywood music, I see those images of Bhara Papa and Dadiji dancing with joy at our wedding. Tara's concern for others is a shadow of the caring that our grandmothers have each individually showered on their children and grandchildren.

And while it aches to lose those who we love so deeply, I can see that their spirits truly never leave us. We hear them in the laughter of our babies and in the rhythm of their footsteps, we see them in the sparkle of our babies' eyes, and we hear them in the meaning behind our babies' words. It is a reincarnation of images, memories, and love that recycles itself over time from one generation to another.

95

I promise to help you
trust your intuition.

Maa, my father's mother, has the most amazing intuition. She astounds those around her over and over again by her insights. She predicted the gender of each one of her grandchildren and great-grandchildren, now eight of them, with complete accuracy. She can look at you and know if something is wrong or something has changed. She is the prototypical mother who has insight, perception, and knowledge.

There is one story about Maa that I will never forget. I had gone with my grandfather, Daddy, for a meeting with his publisher one afternoon when I was living in India. The meeting was taking place in a high-rise office complex in Delhi, and we were packed into the elevator like sardines. Daddy laughed as we both were pushed in a corner, saying that Maa would never enter an elevator because it gave her a sense of claustrophobia. In fact, she would be upset that Daddy would be taking the elevator, rather than walking up the stairs, because she was paranoid about elevators getting stuck.

As the elevator slowly trudged up, there was a sudden jolt, and it stopped.

The electricity in the building had gone off, and we were in between floors. It was an unbearably hot day already, and the body odors around me made me feel nauseated. Daddy remained calm, as he always was, telling me not to fret, that it would just take a few minutes for the generator to come on, and we would be on our way. It took about a half hour, and other than me, everyone else seemed totally unfazed by the whole episode.

Before entering the meeting, Daddy said to me, "Mallika, don't tell Maa about us getting stuck in the elevator. She will be very angry that we took it, and I don't want her to get stressed unnecessarily." He repeated this to me again right before we entered the house, and I promised Daddy that we would keep this our little secret.

When we entered the house, however, we could see that Maa was totally distraught. She immediately asked us, "What happened? Why did you take so long?" Daddy nervously looked at me and told Maa that everything went incredibly well. The meeting was a success, and he started to describe how the publisher had a great plan to promote his book. But Maa would not be distracted. She said, "Don't change the topic. I know something happened. Mallika, what happened?" I, too, replied that nothing had happened. Maa then looked intently at both Daddy and me, closed her eyes for a fraction of a second, and then said, "Something with the elevator . . . Daddy, did you take Mallika in the elevator." I could not believe my ears—how could Maa have known that? And even more surprisingly, while I was so shocked about her insight, it seemed that Daddy wasn't surprised at all. He just laughed, saying, "I never can hide anything from you, can I?" And he began to placate her about the whole adventure, telling her the story and saying that we ended up walking down the stairs on our return.

I later asked Maa about how she was able to know and see things. She looked at me, almost confused, and asked, "How could you not know?" For Maa, she simply asked a question and then listened to the answer. It was very simple. She did not question the answers, she just knew them as truth.

As parents, we play an important role in shaping how our children process information about themselves and their environments. By teaching our children to listen to and trust the answers that are coming from within, we can help build their intuition and give them confidence in their abilities to make decisions.

96

I promise to tell you about angels.

My mother was twenty years old when her closest aunt fell fatally ill. Bimla Aunty was my grandmother's sister, an extremely beautiful woman with a gentle, loving soul.

Bimla Aunty's brother had bought a special life support machine from England and had it shipped to the hospital in Delhi where she was being taken care of. Every day after college, my mother would go to the hospital to sit by her aunt's side; read her the newspaper, philosophy, and poetry; and tell her about the latest gossip in the family or at school.

There was a young resident who worked with Bimla Aunty's doctor. He would come to review her charts every now and then, as well as pay his respects to the various elders who were assembled in the room. It turned out that his mother was also a close friend of Bimla Aunty, and so there was an immediate liking of him. The young resident was my father.

Over the next few months, my father began to visit Bimla Aunty on a regular basis, conveniently arriving at the same time that my mother would come. He would take an extra few minutes every day, telling my mother stories about the Beatles and American movies. By this time, Bimla Aunty was quite sick and could no longer speak. But every time my father entered the door, she would give him a welcoming smile as she squeezed my mother's hand. She served as a silent guardian in their courtship.

And thus my parents love story developed, and they were soon engaged. The first person they told about their engagement was Bimla Aunty, and her eyes sparkled with uninhibited joy.

Bimla Aunty died two months before my parents' wedding, and so they had a quiet ceremony. But although she wasn't physically there, her spirit of grace, elegance, and beauty was ever present. And she is honored as the Angel of Love in our family.

While at times it may be difficult to see them, we are all blessed with angels in our lives. If we are open to their assistance, magical new worlds open for us and those who we love.

Reflection

DO YOU BELIEVE in angels? Think about the people who have made your life magical. Remember to tell your children about them.

97

I promise to show you how to love and feel the spirit of planet earth.

There is a connection between you and the universe that has existed for eternity. You are a being of light, born from the dust of stars and have traveled in different forms through the depths of space and the mystery of time. You are the universe—recycled, regenerated, and reborn millions of times, over and over again.

I want you to see the world as your extended body and love it as you would your own body. The air is your breath. The trees are your lungs. Because they breathe, you and I breathe. The rivers and oceans are your circulation. Their flow, their vitality, and their essence is the energy that has nurtured you through time.

Our bodies are recycled earth, our breath recycled air, our circulation recycled water, our emotions recycled energy, our thoughts recycled information, and our souls a reflection of our other souls.

Know and feel this connection from the depths of your being. Care for the earth as you care for yourself, and she will take care of you. Love the universe with your heart and soul, and it will be in love with you. Talk to the universe, and it will answer your prayers.

98

I promise to help you to see that we are more than just the roles we play.

My father-in-law started traveling to China in the early eighties. He tells amazing stories about his visits because it was a time when China was not really open to the rest of the world. Communism was at its most stringent at those times, and my father-in-law was one of the first Indians who visited the country after years of restrictions because of strife between the two countries.

One of my father-in-law's stories is effective in describing China at that time, but it is also telling in its lessons about perception and preconceived notions.

My father-in-law had a meeting with the Minister of Energy for the Republic of China. It was a very big meeting, and it had the potential to not only create millions of dollars of business for his company but also set a new trade standard for Chinese-Indian trade practices. Thus, my father-in-law had spent months preparing for the meeting and had perfected his proposal for the Minister. On the appointed day, not wanting to be late, he had asked his host to pick him up early to ensure that he would make it to the meeting in good time.

They reached the Ministry of Energy about an hour early. Because my father-in-law was restricted in his access, he decided to wait in the lobby as his host left to get some coffee for him. The lobby was pretty much empty, except for a janitor in a Mao suit who was sweeping the floors and getting the room ready for the day's proceedings. My father-in-law nodded to the janitor, and while the worker returned the smile, he avoided eye contact and remained focused on his work. My father-in-law opened up his briefcase and reviewed his presentation for the big meeting. Soon, his host returned with some coffee and snacks, and they chatted as they passed the time. After half an hour or so, the lobby began to fill up with people heading to work or waiting for meetings with officials in the building.

At the appointed time, my father-in-law was called for his meeting. He was escorted to a conference room in which about twenty other men and women sat, each with pads of paper in front of them and pens in their hands. My father-in-law was seated at one end of the long conference table; the seat at the other end was empty. As my father-in-law sat down, the men and women nodded, and then there was complete silence. His host explained that they were waiting for the Minister to arrive.

In another minute, the door opened. The men and women all stood up, as did my father-in-law. As the Minister sat down at the head of the conference table, my father-in-law had to take a second look. It was none other than the janitor he had just met in the lobby. But now he was dressed in a three-piece suit, and he looked directly into my father-in-law's eyes as he said, "Mr. Mandal. Welcome to the Ministry of Energy."

99

I promise to help you experience the truth in all of its forms.

A group of disciples approached the Buddha to ask his advice on quarrels they were witnessing in the village. They told him about the numerous hermits and holy men in the village who were arguing about the nature of reality. Some argued that the soul dies with the human body, while others claimed it was infinite; some said that God was in human form, while others said that God was infinite and unbounded. There seemed to be no agreement, only bickering, and the disciples were confused about the true nature of reality.

The Buddha told the disciples a story. Once upon a time, an elephant approached a village of blind men. It was the first time that such a creature had come to their town, and the six wisest men pushed the others aside as they set out to discover its nature.

The first blind man felt the elephant's leg and said, "The elephant is like a pillar. Strong and sturdy."

The second blind man felt the elephant's ears and said, "Oh, no. The elephant is like a big wide fan."

The third blind man felt the elephant's tail and said, "The elephant is like a nice, soft, long rope."

The fourth blind man felt the elephant's tusk and said, "You are wrong. The elephant is like a smooth, hard pipe."

The fifth blind man felt the elephant's belly and said, "The elephant is smooth and big like a wall. Nothing can overcome this creature."

The sixth blind man felt the elephant's trunk, and said, "The elephant is like the branch of a tree, strong yet able to swing in the wind."

With each statement, the crowd got louder and louder, and before long the entire village was arguing over the true nature of the elephant. In a matter of minutes, each wise man had a crowd of adamant supporters for his point of view.

The Buddha smiled as he concluded the story. Each man had discovered one aspect of the truth. But it was the collection of all their truths that would give them the sight to really experience the elephant.

100

I promise to help you
discover your unique spirit.

When you were a little seed in my womb, I could feel your body growing inside of me. I talked to you, felt you, and could sense you. But most of all, I could feel your presence, alive and real.

You were born into our world, a tiny infant. Already, you could recognize me as your mother, and with fascination I watched you observe, learn, and become part of this great mystery of existence.

As you grow up, I watch your body develop and your mind sharpen with every interaction. With awe I see your personality bloom as you become an individual with your own voice, opinions, likes, and dislikes. But despite all of these changes, I still can feel your unchanging presence, vibrant and constant as ever.

I see your future as a teenager, becoming a new body with new emotions and a new personality. I can see you as a woman bearing your own children, bringing new life into our world. I witness your personality changing with new experiences, challenges, and opportunities. I feel your pains and joys. I hear your cries and rejoice in your laughter. And I see you as an old woman sitting back in her chair, reflecting on a life of meaningful relationships and accomplishments.

With each new phase of your life, I watch your body, mind, and personality change, but you still remain you. This you is always present is your soul, a divine spark of the infinite spirit that pervades the entire universe.

Your presence has blessed me and made my own spirit soar and dance with ecstasy. I shall love you for eternity, and I am honored that I have been touched by your soul in this lifetime and for lifetimes to come.

The soul is infinite, eternal, unbounded.

Water cannot wet it, fire cannot burn it,

    and weapons cannot shatter it.

Unborn, it does not die with the death of the body.

It is without beginning and without ending.

—FROM THE BHAGAVAD GĪTA